the real Fast Curry COOKBOOK

Other books by Pat Chapman

Curry Club 250 Favourite Curries and Accompaniments

Curry Club 250 Hot and Spicy Dishes

Curry Club Indian Restaurant Cookbook

Curry Club Favourite Restaurant Curries

Curry Club Indian Vegetarian Cookbook

Pat Chapman's Favourite Middle Eastern Recipes

Pat Chapman's Chinese Restaurant Cookbook

Curry Club Balti Curry Cookbook

Curry Club Tandoori and Tikka Dishes

Curry Club Good Curry Restaurant Guide

Curry Club Bangladeshi Restaurant Curries

The New Curry Bible

The Modern Indian Restaurant Cookbook

the real
Fast Curry
COOKBOOK

Pat Chapman

metro

Published by Metro Publishing Ltd,
3, Bramber Court, 2 Bramber Road,
London W14 9PB, England

www.blake.co.uk

First published in paperback in 2005

ISBN 1 84358 149 3

British Library Cataloguing-in-Publication Data:

A catalogue record for this book is available from the British Library.

Design by www.envydesign.co.uk

Printed in Great Britain by CPD

1 3 5 7 9 10 8 6 4 2

Papers used by Metro Publishing are natural, recyclable products made from
wood grown in sustainable forests. The manufacturing processes conform to the
environmental regulations of the country of origin.

CONTENTS

INTRODUCTION

People tell me that they would love to get into curry making. The reason they don't is that they believe it to be too time consuming, and after a busy day's work they haven't the inclination to bother. So they stick with takeaways or rather less satisfying ready-made curries from supermarkets.

Time is precious to everyone, yet curries need not take hours to make. And that's what this book is all about. The recipes will not have you slaving over a hot stove for half the day. They will give you superb quality, delicious tasting, spicy curry dishes with minimal time and effort. And all of them take less than 30 minutes to prepare, from raw to ready. Most take much less time. An entire meal consisting of several recipes can easily be cooked in half an hour. As a matter of fact, they are all recipes which I have been making for as long as I can remember. And even though cooking and recipe-testing is my profession, when it comes to the after-work meal I do not wish to linger in the kitchen any more than any other busy person does.

Some recipes are served cold and require no cooking. Most are cooked on the hob. Because ovens and deep fryers take too long to heat up, I have avoided using them. I have also avoided using blenders and food processors wherever possible. A few recipes use the grill. All the recipes can be prepared without a microwave, but if there is an advantage to be gained by using one I have mentioned this. In a number of recipes I have

1

used easily obtained prepared products – canned items or ready-made salads, for example, and anything which adds flavour but saves time. Dried onion flakes and bottled minced garlic are prime examples. A list of these useful 'short cut' ingredients and the spices you will need for your store cupboard are in Appendix 2, page 115.

Many of the recipes in my other curry books require you to make mixtures, pastes and so on in advance of the main cooking. Here, apart from garam masala and curry and spice powders, I have avoided any pre-preparation. Each recipe stands alone. There are no recipes for Indian breads because most people find them very messy and time-consuming to make.

As to the recipes themselves, you will find many favourite names but you may be surprised at the different, rapid cooking methods. There is nothing 'traditional' here – Indian home-cooking takes hours. And the techniques are not those of the Indian restaurant. Though time is saved, it is not at the expense of taste. As well as your favourite curries you will find a good selection of innovative recipes using ingredients not normally associated with curry. They are well-tried and tested.

The portion size throughout is for two. Halve the ingredient quantities for one person, do one and a half times the amounts for three, double up for four and so on. It will work every time. But enough of these practicalities. Without further ado, let's get on with the cooking!

Pat Chapman
Haslemere

CHAPTER 1

◆

ESSENTIALS

This short chapter is about the all-important spices – and some other ingredients – without which you cannot make curry. So it is essential reading, albeit as brief as I can make it. It also includes the four spice mixtures used in my recipes. Two of them are ground mixtures (known in India as masalas and here as curry powders). One is a straight curry powder, the other a tandoori version. They are quite easy to make and quick to cook. Each recipe that uses them details the cooking process. The third mixture is garam masala, divine when home-made. The fourth, Bengali five spice mixture, is a combination of seeds that is used in certain stir-fries.

You can buy factory-made versions of these mixtures. But my advice is that at the weekend you allocate the spare half hour it will take to make all four of them. The fresh tastes they will give the recipes will be unrivalled by factory-made equivalents. I guarantee that once you have made your own spice mixtures you will always continue to do so.

SPICES

Although the ethos of this book is speed, I have not compromised on the variety of spices you will need to achieve the different tastes in these 100 recipes. Spices are, after all, what curry is all about. The full list is in Appendix 2 on page 115. Even though some spices appear in just a few recipes, it does not cost much to buy all of them. As spices are crucial to all that follows, they should be cared for as if they were gold. There are some rules:

Firstly: Buy in small quantities. Spices deteriorate once their packets are opened and eventually lose all their flavour (or essential oils). Use ground spices within 6–12 months of opening and whole ones within 12–18 months. Beyond those dates, bin them and buy fresh.

Secondly: Store in airtight, lidded containers, in a dry place. Temperature is not important but it is better cooler rather than hotter.

Thirdly: Do not be tempted to display your spices in alluring glass jars in direct sunlight as this fades their colours and, more importantly, diminishes their tastes. Glass containers can be used provided the spices are kept in a dark place, for example in a cupboard or pantry.

Roasting Spices

Some recipes call for roasted whole spices. It is easy to roast them, it's fun and the results are stupendous. The analogy is coffee. The 'roasting' releases those delicious aromatic fragrances, the essential oils, into the air. The simplest way to roast spices is to put them into a pre-heated dry frying pan, wok or karahi and put this on a medium heat on the stove. Dry stir-fry (no oil or water, remember) for 30–60 seconds to release the aromas. Do not let the spices burn. If this happens, bin them – it's cheap enough and quick enough to start again. Cool the spices. You can store them, but it is better to roast them and use them immediately as required.

Grinding Spices

Roast the spices and leave them to cool. Then grind them with a pestle and mortar if you enjoy hard work, or in a coffee grinder or the spice-mill attachment for electric food processors and liquidisers.

FRESH HERBS

Relatively few fresh herbs feature in Indian cooking. Fresh green coriander leaves are the most popular and mint and basil are required in some of the recipes. The most convenient, albeit more expensive, way for after-work cooks to store these herbs so that they are always ready for spontaneous use is to buy ones which grow in pots.

INGREDIENTS

Most of the fresh and dried ingredients in this book are widely available from supermarkets and delicatessens. A list of the dried and specialist 'store cupboard' items you will need, and all the spices used in these recipes, are listed in Appendix 2 on page 115. If you do have problems obtaining items such as ghee, coconut milk, bottled minced coriander, etc., they are available, along with many more ingredients, by mail order.

Garam Masala

—— MAKES 100g (about 7 tablespoons when ground) ——

This is the best example of roasting and grinding your own spices. Please try it at least once. Then compare it with any factory-made garam masala. I guarantee you will do-it-yourself from then on. And it really doesn't take long. Garam means hot and masala means mixture of spices. The heat comes from the black pepper. There are as many mixtures as there are cooks, but all should use aromatic spices. Here is an aromatic version with easy-to-grind spices. Next time you may wish to add other spices or make other changes. Garam masala is often used towards the end of the cooking. Add it too early and you may lose its aromatic qualities. It can also be sprinkled over a finished dish as a garnish. I have used metric quantities for this recipe. Tablespoons (heaped) are acceptable but less accurate. This batch will last you for about ten meals for two. Store the garam masala in an airtight container in a dark place such as a cupboard.

◆

30g (5 tablespoons) coriander seeds
20g (2 tablespoons) white cummin
    seeds
10g (2 tablespoons) fennel seeds
10g (2 inch/5cm piece) cinnamon stick

10g (4–5 pieces) brown cardamom
    pods
10g (2 teaspoons) black peppercorns
10g (2 teaspoons) cloves

◆

1. Mix the spices together in a dry wok or frying pan.

2. Dry stir-fry on medium heat for a minute or so, until a gorgeous aroma is given off.

3. Allow the spices to cool, then grind them as finely as you can.

4. Store in an airtight container.

Home-made Curry Powder

—— MAKES 200g (about 12 tablespoons when ground) ——

Curry powder can be found in every supermarket, the world over. In Britain something like £40 million is spent on it every year. Most cooks have it in their store cupboards although some, it seems, rarely use it. You probably already have a favourite brand and if it is still fresh it will work in any of the recipes that call for curry powder. If it has been there for years it will be stale and tasteless! Six months after you've opened the tub, the contents will be becoming old. It is best to make your own, little and often. Here's a ten spice, easy-to-make mixture, enough for ten double portions – not too little not too much. Again, I have used metric quantities; the spoon measures are good equivalents.

WHOLE SPICES
10g (2 teaspoons) fennel seeds
10g (2 inch/5cm piece) cinnamon stick
10g (2 teaspoons) cloves
3g (4–5) bay leaves

GROUND SPICES
80g (5 tablespoons) ground coriander

35g (2 tablespoons) ground white cummin
30g (2 tablespoons) garam masala (see page 6)
15g (1 tablespoon) paprika
10g (2 teaspoons) turmeric
7g (1½ teaspoons) chilli powder

1. Mix the **whole spices** together in a dry wok or frying pan.

2. Dry stir-fry on medium heat for a minute or so, until a gorgeous aroma is given off.

3. Allow the spices to cool, then grind them as finely as you can.

4. Mix in the **ground spices**.

5. Store in an airtight container.

Tandoori Curry Powder

—— MAKES 200g (about 12 tablespoons when ground) ——

As with all home-made curry powders, this has the advantage of maturing during storage. Keep it in the dark in an airtight container and it will be good for up to 12 months. The bright reds and oranges that we associate with restaurant tandooris and tikkas are phoney, requiring chemical colourings. I have omitted them, but if you want the artificial, restaurant look use 5g (½ teaspoon) red and 3g (⅓ teaspoon) sunset yellow food colouring instead. All spoon measures are heaped.

30g (2 tablespoons) tomato soup powder
30g (2 tablespoons) ground coriander
25g (5 teaspoons) ground cummin
25g (5 teaspoons) garlic powder

25g (5 teaspoons) paprika
20g (4 teaspoons) mango powder
20g (6 teaspoons) dried mint
15g (3 teaspoons) chilli powder
10g (2 teaspoons) salt

1. Simply mix all the ingredients together well and store.

2. Use as described in the recipes.

Bengali Five Spice Mixture

This simple mixture of whole spices is one of Bengal's most popular. Its secret lies in the fact that each of the five spices adds a particular characteristic: fennel (aromatic), fenugreek (bitter), white cummin (savoury), wild onion (sweet), mustard (pungent). Together they are musical.

white cummin seeds
fennel seeds
fenugreek seeds

mustard seeds
wild onion seeds

Simply mix equal quantities together (a teaspoon of each is plenty).

The Quick Curry Meal

Before the recipe section proper, it is worth thinking about what to serve as a quick after-work curry meal; and what to drink with it. In both cases, we are considering everyday eating and drinking.

What to Eat

Preparing these recipes will, I hope, be quick. It does not necessarily follow that the eating must be. True, it can be completely informal – on a tray in front of the television perhaps. But curry meals can just as well be served formally at table or romantically with candlelight and a flower.

Your choice of meal could be just a simple snack or soup on its own, chosen from many of the chapters in this book. Or it could be a full curry with rice (or bread). Or you may like to try my mix-with-rice curry sauces in Chapter 9. For a more elaborate occasion, you may wish to call the snack or soup a 'starter' and follow it with a choice of two curries, rice and chutneys.

What to Drink

The wine drinking habit in Britain continues to grow and it is reasonable to assume that curry eaters wish to drink wine with spicy food. That there is still a little reluctance to do so is the result of years of advice by respected wine critics.

But this is old news, and frankly it is poor advice. David Woolfe, respected wine journalist and Indophile, writing in *The Good Curry Restaurant Guide*, reckons that wine is 'ideal with curry. But since white wines generally have less flavour, it must be red to stand up to the spices and herbs. Most wine books say fine wine is spoiled by chillies. But in my own experience, this is not so. The wine and spices do not argue face to face, but slide past each other. As the wine flavour momentarily takes over the palate "forgets" the chillies; then the chillies return and the wine is forgotten. More likely to spoil the taste of wine is an excess of sweet mango chutney.'

I happen to agree about good red wine, especially when you 'chase' the wine with mineral water. But a dry rosé or sparkling white or pink wine is especially delicious with curry. Beer, on the other hand, can be too filling and too gassy, although 'brewed specially for curry' Cobra lager from Bangalore is excellent. Non-alcoholic drinks are always acceptable.

◆

CHAPTER 2

SALADS, SOUPS AND SNACKS

All the recipes in this chapter are really quick. I have avoided anything that requires long marinating or deep frying. Seven recipes are cold, requiring even less time to make. Hot or cold, they can be enjoyed as snacks at any time, or as a prelude to a main dish.

Bean Sprout Masala Medley

—— SERVES 2 as a snack ——

Many supermarkets and greengrocers now sell attractive packages of mixed bean sprouts. Generally these are green lentils, chick peas, soy beans and yellow lentils. With their mix of shapes and colours as well as their different flavours, these sprouts make a highly nutritious salad. Add spices, and they are heavenly.

5oz (150g) mixed bean sprouts
2 tablespoons cottage cheese
2 tablespoons Greek yoghurt
1 teaspoon very finely diced red
   pepper
1 teaspoon very finely diced green
   pepper

½ teaspoon diced fresh green chilli
2 teaspoons garam masala (see
   page 6)
½ teaspoon home-made curry powder
   (see page 7)
salt to taste

Mix all the ingredients together in a bowl. Chill for up to 24 hours if you have time, or serve at once.

Spicy Spaghetti or Noodles

—— SERVES 2 as a snack ——

What do you do with leftover spaghetti or noodles? This is my super-quick way of making them into an appetizing cold snack. In fact, this recipe is so tasty that it is worth cooking extra spaghetti or noodles for next day use.

---

2 tablespoons hazelnut oil
1 tablespoon olive oil
6oz (175g) cooked and cooled
  spaghetti or egg noodles
1 teaspoon home-made curry powder
  (see page 7)
2 teaspoons garam masala (see
  page 6)

1–3 fresh green chillies, chopped
1 tablespoon chopped fresh green
  coriander leaves
1 tablespoon chopped fresh mint
  leaves
salt to taste

---

1. Pour the oils over the cold spaghetti or noodles and mix in well.

2. Add all the other ingredients, tossing well.

3. Serve on a salad bed with a twist of lemon.

Variation Add shredded cooked beef, chopped chicken or small shrimps at Stage 2.

Spicy Cottage Cheese

—— **SERVES** 2 as part of a meal ——

India's cheese is called paneer. Our cottage cheese is similar, though saltier. Here is a simple, virtually instant and very tasty cold snack. Serve with salads and cold dishes from this chapter, or as a sandwich spread.

◆

5oz (150g) cottage cheese
2 teaspoons garam masala
1 fresh green chilli, chopped (optional)

◆

Mix all the ingredients together in a bowl. Chill for up to 24 hours if you have time, or serve at once.

Spiced Shredded Vegetable Salad

—— SERVES 2 as part of meal ——

Supermarkets these days offer mouthwatering, ready-prepared salads which save time and wastage. This recipe elevates humble shredded carrot and cabbage (coleslaw minus the salad cream), other mixed green salad leaves and spring onions to something special. You could choose other salad options if you wish.

2oz (50g) mixed green salad leaves
   such as watercress, lettuce, spinach
3–4 spring onions (leaves and bulbs)
5oz (150g) shredded carrot and
   cabbage mixture
1 fresh red chilli, chopped (optional)
2 tablespoons olive oil

1 tablespoon sunflower oil
2 tablespoons fresh lemon or lime juice
2 teaspoons garam masala (see
   page 6)
1 teaspoon home-made curry powder
   (see page 7)
salt to taste

---

1. Shred the green leaves and spring onions.

2. Mix all the ingredients together in a bowl. Chill for an hour or two if you have time, or serve at once.

Kashmiri Salad

—— SERVES 2 as part of a meal ——

A quick and quite delicious combination of salad vegetables linked together with yoghurt, spices and a hint of mayonnaise.

4–6 spring onions (leaves and bulbs), chopped
4–6 radicchio leaves, shredded
1 tablespoon shredded red pepper
1–2 tomatoes, chopped
1–2 fresh green chillies, chopped
1 tablespoon chopped cooked beetroot in vinegar

1 tablespoon garam masala (see page 6)
3–4 tablespoons Greek yoghurt
2–3 teaspoons mayonnaise
salt to taste

Mix all the ingredients together in a non-metallic bowl. Chill for up to 6 hours if you have time, or serve at once.

Curried Rice Salad

—— SERVES 2 as a snack ——

Curried rice salad is particularly delicious, and is quick to make. Here I have included some especially tasty enhancements such as cummin seeds, fresh garam masala and chillies.

◆

½ lb (225g) cooked and cooled basmati rice
½ teaspoon white cummin seeds
1 tablespoon pistachio nut oil
2–3 spring onions (bulbs and leaves), chopped
1–2 fresh red chillies, chopped
6 tablespoons Greek yoghurt
1 tablespoon mayonnaise

1 tablespoon home-made curry powder (see page 7) or tandoori curry powder (see page 8)
1 teaspoon garam masala (see page 6)
salt to taste

GARNISH
chopped pistachio nuts
fresh green coriander leaves

◆

Mix all the ingredients together in a bowl. Chill if you have time, or serve at once.

Curried Pâté

—— SERVES 2 ——

This really works well and is so easy! Serve on hot buttered toast (or with hot naan bread) and with one of the salads in this chapter.

◆

4oz (110g) pâté (any type)
2 teaspoons garam masala (see page 6)
½ teaspoon chilli powder (optional)

◆

1. Simply decant any pâté of your choice into a bowl, discarding any aspic or skin.
2. Mix in the remaining ingredients.

Chilled Pepper Water

—— SERVES 2 ——

If you happen to adore tomato juice with a drop or three of Worcestershire sauce, as I do, you will enjoy this as a fantastically refreshing alternative, on hot summer evenings perhaps – or at any time.

◆

2 teaspoons soya or sunflower oil

SPICES
1 teaspoon ground coriander
½ teaspoon ground cummin
⅓ teaspoon mango powder
½–1 teaspoon chilli powder

12fl oz (350ml) cold vegetable stock or water
4fl oz (100ml) tomato juice
½ teaspoon Worcestershire sauce
1 tablespoon finely chopped fresh mint leaves
salt to taste

◆

1. Heat the oil in a frying pan. Add the **spices** and stir-fry for about 30 seconds. Remove the pan from the heat.

2. Add some of the vegetable stock or water to the pan and swill the spices out into a bowl. Add the remaining stock or water, the tomato juice, Worcestershire sauce, mint leaves and salt to taste.

3. Put some crushed ice into 2 highball glasses and pour pepper water into each one, stirring it as you do so.

Popadoms

—— ALLOW 2–3 per person ——

Popadoms are the most satisfying of all preludes to an Indian meal. I like to munch my way through them accompanied by at least one chutney (see Chapter 11) while I cook my main curry meal. Deep frying takes rather too long if time is pressing, so here are two quick ways to cook popadoms.

The Grill

Set the heat to about three-quarters and the grill tray midway from the heat. Grill 1–2 popadoms at a time for about 10 seconds. Ensure that the edges are cooked. Because they are oil-free they can be served at once or stored until ready.

The Microwave

Popadoms can also be microwaved. Most machines are power-rated at 650 watts. Put in 2 popadoms and cook on full power for about 30 seconds. Inspect and apply more heat if necessary. Serve at once or store until needed.

Prawn Patia

—— SERVES 2 as a starter ——

Slightly sweet, yet contrastingly hot and tangy, patia is a good stir-fry starter. Serve with bread rolls, lemon wedges and a side salad.

◆

2 tablespoons ghee or vegetable oil
½ teaspoon white cummin seeds
½ teaspoon fennel seeds
2 teaspoons minced bottled garlic
1 tablespoon home-made curry powder (see page 7)
1 tablespoon tandoori curry powder (see page 8)
6 tablespoons dried onion flakes
8–10oz (225–300g) thawed small, cooked, shelled prawns

1 tablespoon tomato ketchup
1 tablespoon tomato purée
1 tablespoon coconut milk powder
1 tablespoon brown sugar
2 teaspoons prawn ballichow (optional)
½ teaspoon bottled minced coriander
salt to taste

◆

1. Heat the ghee or oil in a frying pan and stir-fry the seeds for 10 seconds. Add the garlic and continue stir-frying for about a minute. Add the curry and tandoori curry powders and stir-fry for a further minute.

2. Now add the onion flakes, stirring briskly until they absorb the oil and start sizzling. Add about 3½fl oz (100ml) water and bring to a simmer.

3. Add the prawns and all the remaining ingredients except the salt. Simmer gently for 5 minutes or so, during which time the sauce will thicken up nicely. Add salt to taste.

4. Serve piping hot.

Variation Prawn Patia is excellent served on popadoms instead of with bread rolls. Cook the popadoms during stage 3 of the patia recipe and simply put the hot patia on them just prior to serving (too early and the popadoms will go soggy). Serve with chutneys.

Spicy Potato Rissoles

—— MAKES 4 rissoles ——

The name of the game here is to use up cooked potatoes. Mashed, spiced and shallow fried, they are transformed into delicious rissoles. Serve with pickles and a salad.

◆

4–6 large potatoes, cooked
1–2 teaspoons home-made curry
  powder (see page 7)
1 teaspoon bottled minced garlic
1 teaspoon white cummin seeds
1–3 fresh green chillies, finely chopped
1 tablespoon chopped fresh green
  coriander leaves

½ teaspoon salt
milk or water
1 egg
4–6 tablespoons breadcrumbs
4 tablespoons vegetable oil

◆

1. Mash the potatoes with the curry powder, garlic, cummin seeds, chilli, fresh coriander and salt. If the mixture is too dry to cohere, add just enough milk or water to achieve this.

2. Divide the mixture into 4 balls. Shape each ball into a flat round or sausage shape.

3. Whisk the egg with a fork in a small bowl. Spread the breadcrumbs on a chopping board.

4. Coat the potato rissoles with the egg then cover them with the breadcrumbs.

5. Heat the oil in a frying pan and fry the rissoles for about 5 minutes, turning them frequently.

6. Serve hot (or cold).

Variations   Add 2 or 3 tablespoons each of peas and/or chopped ham during Stage 1.

Spicy Tomato Soup

—— SERVES 2 ——

This is so simple, you could call it cheating! I have it whenever I can. You simply open the can, heat the soup and add the spices. You can substitute packet (dry mix) tomato soup for the canned version; follow the packet instructions to re-constitute.

1 × 14fl oz (400ml) can cream of
   tomato soup
1 tablespoon vinegar (any type)
1 teaspoon Worcestershire sauce

SPICES
⅓ teaspoon ground cummin
⅓ teaspoon ground coriander
½ teaspoon garam masala (see page 6)

½ teaspoon chilli powder (optional)
salt to taste

GARNISH
a curl of single cream
snipped chives or dill, or fresh
   coriander leaves

1. Heat the soup in a saucepan.

2. Mix the **spices** with the vinegar and Worcestershire sauce in a bowl.

3. Add the spice mixture to the soup and bring to a simmer. Add salt to taste and serve garnished with the cream and fresh herbs.

Spicy Tomato Juice

—— SERVES 2 ——

This lighter version of the previous recipe uses tomato juice with the same spicing. It can be served hot or cold.

◆

1 tablespoon vinegar (any type)
1 teaspoon Worcestershire sauce
14fl oz (400ml) bottled or tetrapack
   tomato juice
salt to taste

SPICES
⅓ teaspoon ground cummin
⅓ teaspoon ground coriander
½ teaspoon garam masala (see page 6)
½ teaspoon chilli powder (optional)

◆

1. Mix the **spices** with the vinegar and Worcestershire sauce and mix with the tomato juice. Add salt to taste.

2. Heat in a saucepan, stirring well, and serve hot, or add ice, preferably crushed, before serving chilled.

Vegetable Rasam Soup

—— SERVES 2 ——

This is an imaginative and easy way to use up vegetable leftovers and bits and pieces in the fridge.

◆

2 tablespoons vegetable ghee or
  sesame oil
½ teaspoon white cummin seeds
½ teaspoon mustard seeds
½ teaspoon sesame seeds
1–2 teaspoons bottled minced garlic
2 teaspoons home-made curry powder
  (see page 7)

About 3oz (75g) mixed cooked
  vegetables, chopped small
2 tablespoons chopped fresh green
  coriander leaves
10–12 curry leaves, fresh or dried
1–2 fresh red chillies, chopped
  (optional)
salt to taste

◆

1. Heat the ghee or oil in a saucepan. Stir-fry the seeds for 20 seconds. Add the garlic and curry powder and stir-fry for 1 minute.

2. Add 14fl oz (400ml) water and bring to a simmer.

3. Add the vegetables, fresh coriander, curry leaves and the chilli if using and bring to a simmer. Add salt to taste, strain if you wish, and serve hot.

CHAPTER 3

◆

INSTANT TANDOORIS
AND TIKKAS

Here is a totally new approach to tandooris and tikkas, which normally need to be marinated for a day or two – and who thinks that far ahead in a busy working week? I could often kill for a tandoori or tikka 'off the peg', so to speak, and so these are my 'instant' non-marinated versions which are almost indistinguishable from the 60-hour ones! If you are particularly fond of tandoori and tikka, you may wish to obtain my book *100 Favourite Tandoori Recipes*.

Instant Meat Tikka

—— SERVES 2 as a snack ——

Pieces of meat are traditionally marinated, then skewered and baked. This recipe dispenses with the marinade and because the meat is cut into tiny pieces it can be stir-fried to achieve almost as good a result in a fraction of the time. Serve with a side salad and raita.

◆

3 tablespoons vegetable oil
2 teaspoons bottled minced garlic
2 tablespoons tandoori curry powder
  (see page 8)
2 tablespoons tomato purée

10–12oz (300–350g) minute steak, cut
  into approx. 8 × 8 mm × 5 cm
  (⅓ × ⅓ × 2 inch) strips
⅓ teaspoon garam masala (see page 6)
⅓ teaspoon salt

◆

1. Heat the oil in a wok or karahi. Stir-fry the garlic for 20 seconds, then add the tandoori curry powder, continuing to stir-fry briskly for one more minute. Add 3 tablespoons water, mixing it in well, then add the tomato purée.

2. Add the strips of meat, turning them over and over in the mixture, and stir-fry for 3–5 minutes depending on whether you like your meat rare or well cooked.

3. Sprinkle on the garam masala and salt and serve.

Grilled Tandoori Chops

—— SERVES 2 ——

This is one of the few recipes in this book that requires the grill. The chops are coated and grilled, and immediately enjoyed with a side salad and a chutney.

4 lamb or pork chops, each weighing
  4oz (110g)
2oz (50g) Greek yoghurt
1 tablespoon vegetable oil
1 tablespoon bottled lemon juice
1 teaspoon bottled minced garlic
½ teaspoon chilli powder

½ teaspoon garam masala (see
  page 6)
1 tablespoon tandoori curry powder
  (see page 8)
1 tablespoon tomato purée
¼ teaspoon salt
4 tablespoons milk

1. Trim some, but not all, excess fat from the chops and make small gashes in the meat with a sharp knife.

2. Mix all the remaining ingredients into a paste in a non-metallic bowl.

3. Immerse the chops in the paste, ensuring they are well coated.

4. Preheat the grill to medium and line the grill tray with foil. Put the rack over it and the coated chops on the rack. Place the tray midway from the heat and grill the chops for about 5 minutes.

5. Turn the chops over and baste them with any spare paste. Grill for a minimum of another 3 minutes or until properly cooked.

Instant Chicken Tikka

—— SERVES 2 ——

As with the recipe for Instant Meat Tikka (see page 25) this dry stir-fry one, for chicken, omits the traditional marinating, skewering and baking and gives an instant (well, almost instant – 10 to 15 minutes as opposed to hours) result. Serve with salads, bread and a chutney or two. Note the use of wine, if you happen to have some to hand – which is advisable to fortify the 'after-work' cook.

◆

10–12oz (300–350g) boned chicken
  breasts, skinned
2 tablespoons vegetable oil
2 teaspoons bottled minced garlic
2 tablespoons tandoori curry powder
  (see page 8)

2 tablespoons tomato purée
⅓ teaspoon salt
red wine (optional)

◆

1. Cut the chicken into bite-sized pieces about 1¼ inches (3.25cm) square.

2. Mix all the remaining ingredients together in a large bowl, then add the chicken pieces, ensuring they are well coated.

3. Heat a wok or large frying pan. Add the contents of the bowl and stir-fry on medium heat until the chicken is cooked (between 10 and 15 minutes). If it begins to dry up, causing sticking and smoking, add a tablespoon or two of water or red wine from time to time.

King Prawn Tikka

—— **SERVES 2** ——

The previous recipe works equally well for prawns. You can use any size with equal success, but allow less frying time for smaller prawns and more for larger.

12oz (350g) shelled prawns (any size), weighed after thawing

2 tablespoons vegetable oil

2 teaspoons bottled minced garlic

2 tablespoons tandoori curry powder (see page 8)

2 tablespoons tomato purée

½ teaspoon salt

---

1. Remove any veins from the prawns' backs. Wash and dry the prawns.

2. Mix all the remaining ingredients in a large bowl, then add the prawns ensuring they are well coated.

3. Heat a wok or large frying pan. Add the contents of the bowl and stir-fry on medium heat until the prawns are cooked (8–10 minutes).

Tandoori Herring

—— SERVES 2 ——

Coat the herrings with a yoghurt-based tandoori-flavoured coating and grill them. Then serve with salad, lemon wedges, bread or a rice dish and chutneys. If you happen to be contemplating a summer barbecue ...

---

2 fresh herrings, each weighing about
   12oz (350g)
5oz (150g) Greek yoghurt
2 tablespoons tandoori curry powder
   (see page 8)

2 tablespoons tomato purée
1 teaspoon salt

---

1. Gut and wash the herrings and dry them.

2. Mix the other ingredients together in a bowl, then coat the herrings with most of the mixture.

3. Preheat the grill to three-quarters of its maximum heat and line the grill tray with foil. Put the rack over it and the coated herrings on the rack. Place the tray midway from the heat and grill the herrings for about 10–12 minutes. Turn them at least once and baste with the remaining spice mixture.

4. To finish off, raise the tray nearer the heat to singe the herrings so that they blacken slightly.

Rapid Chicken Tikka Masala Curry

—— SERVES 2 ——

Chicken Tikka Masala has become the nation's favourite curry. It is tangy rather than hot, savoury and a touch sweet, creamy and colourful. This version is an extension of the Instant Chicken Tikka (see page 27). You simply create a gravy while you cook the stir-fry. Serve with a rice dish. Please don't be put off by the long list of ingredients. Once assembled, the whole curry takes only 15 minutes to cook. Here's how.

◆

12oz (350g) boned chicken breasts, skinned

COATING
2 tablespoons vegetable oil
1 tablespoon tandoori curry powder (see page 8)
2 tablespoons tomato purée
3 tablespoons Greek yoghurt

SAUCE
2 tablespoons vegetable or butter ghee or vegetable oil
½ teaspoon white cummin seeds
½ teaspoon black mustard seeds
1 tablespoon tandoori curry powder (see page 8)
2 teaspoons home-made curry powder (see page 7)
2 teaspoons bottled minced garlic
3 tablespoons dried onion flakes

1 teaspoon dried fenugreek leaves (optional)
1 teaspoon dried mint leaves (optional)
2–3 canned plum tomatoes, chopped
6–8 tablespoons canned cream of tomato soup
1 tablespoon chopped red pepper
1 tablespoon chopped green pepper
1–2 fresh green chillies, chopped
2fl oz (50ml) single cream
1oz (25g) creamed coconut, chopped
1 teaspoon garam masala (see page 6)
1 teaspoon sugar
1 tablespoon chopped fresh green coriander leaves

GARNISH
a curl of single cream
fresh green coriander leaves
flaked almonds

◆

1. Cut the chicken pieces into 1½ inch (3.75cm) cubes.

2. Mix the coating ingredients together in a large bowl, then add the chicken pieces ensuring they are well coated.

3. Heat a wok or large frying pan. Add the contents of the bowl and stir-fry for about 8–10 minutes.

4. Meanwhile, in a separate pan, heat the ghee or vegetable oil and stir-fry the seeds and curry powders for 20 seconds. Add the garlic and continue to stir-fry for a further 30 seconds. Add the onion flakes, fenugreek and mint and stir-fry briskly. The flakes will absorb the oil quickly and could start burning. Before they do, add the tomatoes and tomato soup, then bring to a simmer and add the peppers and chilli. Simmer for about 5 minutes. If it seems too dry at any time, add a little water to keep things mobile.

5. Add this mixture to the contents of the wok, then add the remaining ingredients. Stir-fry for about 5 minutes, then garnish with the cream, coriander leaves and flaked almonds.

Rapid Meat Tikka Masala Curry

—— SERVES 2 ——

Like the previous recipe, this one cooks fast (15 minutes). It is an extension of the Instant Meat Tikka on page 25. Note the good cut of meat, which avoids gristle and achieves tenderness more quickly than cheap cuts. Serve with a rice dish.

12oz (350g) fat-free rump or fillet steak

COATING

2 tablespoons vegetable oil

1 tablespoon tandoori curry powder (see page 8)

2 tablespoons tomato purée

3 tablespoons Greek yoghurt

SAUCE

2 tablespoons vegetable or butler ghee or vegetable oil

½ teaspoon white cummin seeds

½ teaspoon black mustard seeds

1 tablespoon tandoori curry powder (see page 8)

2 teaspoons home-made curry powder (see page 7)

2 teaspoons bottled minced garlic

3 tablespoons dried onion flakes

1 teaspoon dried fenugreek leaves (optional)

1 teaspoon dried mint leaves (optional)

2–3 canned plum tomatoes, chopped

6–8 tablespoons canned cream of tomato soup

1 tablespoon chopped red pepper

1 tablespoon chopped green pepper

1–2 fresh green chillies, chopped

2fl oz (50ml) single cream

1oz (25g) creamed coconut, chopped

1 teaspoon garam masala (see page 6)

1 teaspoon sugar

1 tablespoon chopped fresh green coriander leaves

GARNISH

a curl of single cream

fresh green coriander leaves

flaked almonds

---

1. Cut the steak into 1 × ½ × ½ inch (2.5 × 1.3 × 1.3cm) cubes.

2. Mix the coating ingredients together in a large bowl, then add the meat ensuring it is well coated.

3. Heat a wok or large frying pan. Add the contents of the bowl and stir-fry for about 6–8 minutes.

4. Meanwhile, in a separate pan, heat the ghee or vegetable oil and stir-fry the seeds and curry powders for 20 seconds. Add the garlic and

continue to stir-fry for a further 30 seconds. Add the onion flakes, fenugreek and mint and stir-fry briskly. The flakes will absorb the oil quickly and could start burning. Before they do, add the tomatoes and tomato soup, then bring to a simmer and add peppers and the chilli. Simmer for about 5 minutes. If it becomes a little dry, add just enough water to keep things mobile.

5. Add this mixture to the contents of the wok, then add the remaining ingredients. Stir-fry for about 5 minutes, then garnish with the cream, coriander leaves and flaked almonds.

Rapid Prawn Tikka Masala Curry

—— SERVES 2 ——

Like the previous two recipes, this one is fast to cook. Use king prawns or, if you like, a mixture of king and ordinary prawns. My cooking times are for uncooked, thawed, peeled ones. If you use cooked prawns reduce the cooking time of Step 3 to 2–3 minutes. Serve with rice.

◆

12–14oz (350–400g) peeled, uncooked king prawns

COATING
2 tablespoons vegetable oil
1 tablespoon tandoori curry powder (see page 8)
2 tablespoons tomato purée
3 tablespoons Greek yoghurt

SAUCE
2 tablespoons ghee or vegetable oil
½ teaspoon white cummin seeds
½ teaspoon black mustard seeds
1 tablespoon tandoori curry powder (see page 8)
2 teaspoons home-made curry powder (see page 7)
2 teaspoons bottled minced garlic
1 teaspoon dried fenugreek leaves (optional)

1 teaspoon dried mint leaves (optional)
3 tablespoons dried onion flakes
2–3 canned plum tomatoes, chopped
6–8 tablespoons canned cream of tomato soup
1 tablespoon chopped red pepper
1 tablespoon chopped green pepper
1–2 fresh green chillies, chopped
2fl oz (50ml) single cream
1 oz (25g) creamed coconut, chopped
1 teaspoon garam masala (see page 6)
1 teaspoon sugar
1 tablespoon chopped fresh green coriander leaves

GARNISH
a curl of single cream
fresh green coriander leaves
flaked almonds

◆

1. Remove any veins from the prawns' backs. Wash and dry the prawns.

2. Mix the coating ingredients together in a large bowl, then add the prawns ensuring they are well coated.

3. Heat a wok or large frying pan. Add the contents of the bowl and stir-fry for about 6–8 minutes.

4. Meanwhile, in a separate pan, heat the ghee or vegetable oil and stir-fry the seeds and curry powders for 20 seconds. Add the garlic and continue to stir-fry for a further 30 seconds. Add the onion flakes,

fenugreek and mint and stir-fry briskly. The flakes will absorb the oil quickly and could start burning. Before they do, add the tomatoes and tomato soup, then bring to a simmer and add the peppers and chillies. Simmer for about 5 minutes. If it gets too dry, add just enough water, little by little, to keep things mobile.

5. Add this mixture to the contents of the wok, then add the remaining ingredients. Stir-fry for about 5 minutes, then garnish with the cream, coriander leaves and flaked almonds.

Chicken Tikka Omelette

—— SERVES 2 ——

This combines the chicken and the egg in a novel way. I first came across it at the Titash restaurant in Sheldon, Birmingham. I suggest you make this omelette when you have a little spare leftover chicken tikka in the fridge. Serve with salad and fresh rolls or chips.

◆

4 large free-range eggs
fresh red chilli, chopped, to taste
1 tablespoon chopped fresh green
    coriander leaves
freshly ground black pepper to taste
⅓ teaspoon salt

3–4oz (75–100g) cooked chicken tikka
butter for frying

GARNISH

snipped chives
garam masala (see page 6)

◆

1. Whisk the eggs in a bowl. Add the chilli, fresh coriander, pepper to taste and salt, mixing well.

2. Chop the chicken tikka into small pieces.

3. Heat the tikka by stir-frying it quickly until it is hot right through (or by microwaving it).

4. Heat a dab of butter in a frying pan. When it has melted pour off the excess into another pan.

5. Give the egg mixture a final brisk whisk, then pour half of it into the frying pan. Deftly roll the egg mixture around the pan with a quick wrist action. Return to the heat. When it begins to set, add half the hot chicken tikka.

6. Cook for about one more minute, then slide the omelette out of the pan, roll it up and keep it warm.

7. Repeat Steps 5 and 6 to cook the second omelette.

8. Garnish with the chives and garam masala.

CHAPTER 4

INSTANT BALTIS

Balti curries have taken the nation by storm. Originally slow-cooked dishes from the northernmost part of Pakistan, they evolved via Birmingham into rapid stir-fries (so are most suitable for this book). They are cooked and served in a two-handled pan – the balti pan or karahi – and eaten with naan bread. If you have such a pan it adds to the fun. Use a 10 inch (25cm) balti pan, serve out of it and eat with warm pitta or naan bread and chutneys. Baltiholics, or potential converts to the delights of balti, may wish to obtain my book *The Balti Curry Cookbook*, published by Piatkus, which goes into the subject in great depth.

Balti Meat

—— SERVES 2 as a main course ——

Normally meat needs a long, slow cook to become tender. Here the time is minimised by using rump or fillet steak and cutting it relatively thinly.

◆

12–14oz (350–400g) rump or fillet steak

4 tablespoons butter ghee or vegetable oil

½ teaspoon white cummin seeds

½ teaspoon fennel seeds

¼ teaspoon green cardamom seeds

2 teaspoons bottled minced garlic

1 teaspoon bottled minced ginger

1 tablespoon home-made curry powder (see page 7)

1 tablespoon garam masala (see page 6)

6 tablespoons dried onion flakes

3fl oz (75ml) tomato juice

2fl oz (50ml) red wine (optional)

1 tablespoon chopped red pepper

1 fresh green chilli, chopped (optional); use more if you wish

1 teaspoon dried fenugreek leaves

2 tablespoons Greek yoghurt

1 tablespoon chopped fresh green coriander leaves

salt to taste

GARNISH

fresh green coriander leaves

◆

1. Cut the steak into 1 × ½ × ½ inch (2.5 × 1.3 × 1.3 cm) pieces.

2. Heat half the ghee or oil in a balti pan, wok or large frying pan. Stir-fry the seeds for 20 seconds. Add the garlic and ginger and continue to stir-fry for 30 seconds more. Add the remaining ghee or oil and the curry powder and garam masala.

3. Add the onion flakes and stir-fry briskly. They will absorb the oil quickly and could start burning. Before they do, add the tomato juice, and the red wine if using or 50 ml (2 fl oz) water. Bring to a simmer and add the meat, peppers, chilli if using and fenugreek leaves.

4. Keep on stir-frying for about 5 minutes, then add the yoghurt and fresh coriander.

5. Continue stir-frying until the meat reaches the tenderness you like (at least another 5 minutes). Watch the liquid balance. The mixture should not be dry nor should it be swamped; you will probably need to add a tablespoon of water from time to time.

6. Add salt to taste, garnish with the coriander leaves and serve.

Balti Chicken

—— SERVES 2 as a main course ——

Chicken suits the stir-fry process well. It will cook to succulence in no more than 15 minutes, so why not in the same time make it into really tasty balti? Serve from the pan with naan or pitta bread and chutneys.

12–14oz (350–400g) boned chicken breasts or legs, skinned

4 tablespoons butter ghee or vegetable oil

½ teaspoon white cummin seeds

½ teaspoon fennel seeds

¼ teaspoon green cardamom seeds

2 teaspoons bottled minced garlic

1 teaspoon bottled minced ginger

1 tablespoon home-made curry powder (see page 7)

1 tablespoon garam masala (see page 6)

6 tablespoons dried onion flakes

3fl oz (75ml) tomato juice

2fl oz (50ml) red wine (optional)

1 tablespoon chopped red pepper

1 fresh green chilli, chopped (optional); use more if you wish

1 teaspoon dried fenugreek leaves

2 tablespoons Greek yoghurt

1 tablespoon chopped fresh green coriander leaves

salt to taste

Garnish
fresh green coriander leaves

---

1. Cut the chicken into bite-sized (about 1¼ inch/3.25cm) pieces.

2. Heat half the ghee or oil in a balti pan, wok or large frying pan. Stir-fry the seeds for 20 seconds. Add the garlic and ginger and continue to stir-fry for 30 seconds more. Add the remaining ghee or oil and the curry powder and garam masala.

3. Add the onion flakes and stir-fry briskly. They will absorb the oil quickly and could start burning. Before they do, add the tomato juice, and the red wine if using or 2fl oz (50ml) water. Bring to a simmer and add the chicken, peppers, chilli if using and fenugreek leaves.

4. Keep on stir-frying for about 5 minutes, then add the yoghurt and fresh coriander.

5. Continue stir-frying until the chicken is cooked (about another 10 minutes). The mixture should not be dry nor should it be swamped; you will probably need to add a tablespoon of water from time to time.

6. Add salt to taste, garnish with the coriander leaves and serve.

Balti Fish

—— SERVES 2 as a main course ——

Cod or haddock steaks are ideal balti subjects. They are easily obtainable, inexpensive and stir-fry well, by which I mean they cook quickly and do not break up.

12–14oz (350–400g) cod or haddock
  steaks, filleted
3 tablespoons soya or sunflower oil
½ teaspoon fennel seeds
½ teaspoon black mustard seeds
¼ teaspoon lovage seeds (optional)
3 teaspoons bottled minced garlic
2½ teaspoons home-made curry
  powder (see page 7)
½ teaspoon turmeric
1 tablespoon garam masala (see page
  6)
6 tablespoons dried onion flakes

3fl oz (75ml) milk
1oz (25g) creamed coconut, chopped
1 tablespoon chopped green pepper
1 fresh red chilli, chopped (optional);
  use more if you wish
2 tablespoons single cream
1 tablespoon chopped fresh green
  coriander leaves
salt to taste

GARNISH
fresh green coriander leaves
desiccated coconut

---

1. Cut the fish into pieces about 1 inch (2.5cm) square.

2. Heat half the oil in a balti pan, wok or large frying pan. Stir-fry the seeds for 20 seconds. Add the garlic and stir-fry for 30 seconds. Add the remaining oil, the curry powder, turmeric and garam masala.

3. Add the onion flakes and stir-fry briskly. They will absorb the oil quickly and could start burning. Before they do, add the milk and creamed coconut. Bring to a simmer and add the fish, pepper and chilli if using.

4. Keep on stir-frying for about 5 minutes, then add the cream and fresh coriander.

5. Continue stir-frying for about another 5 minutes until the fish is cooked right through. Watch the liquid balance. The mixture should not be dry nor should it be swamped; you will probably need to add a tablespoon of water from time to time.

6. Add salt to taste, garnish with the coriander leaves and coconut.

Balti Prawns

—— SERVES 2 as a main course ——

Use small, thawed, cooked, peeled prawns for this receipe. Avoid cheap ones because they lose a lot of weight when thawed (they are sprayed with water which adds weight when frozen). The given weight (below) is after thawing.

---

3 tablespoons soya or sunflower oil
½ teaspoon fennel seeds
½ teaspoon black mustard seeds
¼ teaspoon lovage seeds (optional)
3 teaspoons bottled minced garlic
2½ teaspoons home-made curry powder (see page 7)
½ teaspoon turmeric
1 tablespoon garam masala (see page 6)
6 tablespoons dried onion flakes
1oz (25g) creamed coconut, chopped
3fl oz (75ml) milk

14oz (400g) small, cooked, peeled prawns
1 tablespoon chopped green pepper
1 or more fresh red chillies, chopped
½ teaspoon dried fenugreek leaves
2 tablespoons single cream
1 tablespoon chopped fresh green coriander leaves
salt to taste

GARNISH
fresh green coriander leaves
desiccated coconut

---

1. Heat half the oil in a balti pan, wok or large frying pan. Stir-fry the seeds for 20 seconds. Add the garlic and continue to stir-fry for 30 seconds more. Add the remaining oil and the curry powder, turmeric and garam masala.

2. Add the onion flakes and stir-fry briskly. They will absorb the oil quickly and could start burning. Before they do, add the creamed coconut and milk. Bring to a simmer and add the prawns, pepper, chilli and fenugreek leaves.

3. Keep on stir-frying for about 5 minutes, then add the cream and fresh coriander.

4. Continue stir-frying for about another 5 minutes until the prawns are cooked right through. Watch the liquid balance. The mixture should not be dry nor should it be swamped; you will probably need to add a tablespoon of water from time to time.

5. Add salt to taste, garnish with the coriander leaves and coconut.

Balti Vegetables

—— SERVES 2 as a main course ——

The fun thing about balti is that you can combine anything with anything. The next four recipes give some examples. Here I use a combination of vegetables which are all quick to cook, including canned potatoes. It is a good recipe for using up leftover vegetables in the fridge.

◆

3oz (75g) celery

3oz (75g) mange tout

3oz (75g) carrots

3–4 canned or cooked potatoes

3–4 cherry tomatoes

3oz (75g) peas

3 tablespoons vegetable oil

1 teaspoon white cummin seeds

2 teaspoons bottled minced garlic

1 tablespoon home-made curry
  powder (see page 7)

6 tablespoons dried onion flakes

3fl oz (75ml) tomato juice

1 tablespoon chopped red pepper

1 fresh green chilli, chopped; use more
  if you wish

1 teaspoon dried fenugreek leaves

2 tablespoons Greek yoghurt

1 teaspoon garam masala (see page 6)

2 teaspoons chopped fresh green
  coriander leaves

salt to taste

GARNISH

fresh green coriander leaves

shredded carrot

◆

1. Wash and prepare the vegetables. Cut the celery into small pieces, top and tail the mange tout, slice the carrots, quarter the potatoes and halve the tomatoes.

2. Heat the oil in a balti pan, wok or frying pan. Stir-fry the cummin seeds for 20 seconds, add the garlic and stir-fry for a further 30 seconds. Add the curry powder and a tablespoon or two of water and stir-fry for a further minute.

3. Add the onion flakes and stir-fry briskly. They will absorb the oil quickly. Before they start burning, add the tomato juice. Bring to a simmer and add the vegetables, pepper, chilli and fenugreek leaves.

4. Keep on stir-frying for about 3 minutes, then add the yoghurt, garam masala and fresh coriander.

5. Continue to stir-fry for a further 2–3 minutes, adding a little water if necessary to prevent sticking.

6. Add salt to taste, garnish with the coriander leaves and carrot.

Balti Sweetcorn and Mushroom Stir-Fry

—— SERVES 2 as a starter ——

Canned sweetcorn kernels have a gorgeous flavour and are 'instant' to use. Fresh mushrooms bring the dish alive. The balti flavour comes from the combination of curry powder and aromatic garam masala. Serve with packet pitta bread which you've heated in a toaster or under the grill, lemon wedges and a side salad.

◆

½ lb (225g) canned sweetcorn kernels

2 tablespoons vegetable ghee or sesame oil

½ teaspoon white cummin seeds

½ teaspoon fennel seeds

2 teaspoons bottled minced garlic

1 teaspoon bottled minced ginger

1 tablespoon home-made curry powder (see page 7)

1 tablespoon garam masala (see page 6)

2 tablespoons dried onion flakes

6oz (175g) mushrooms (any type), chopped or sliced

4–6 spring onions (bulbs and leaves), chopped

2–3 canned tomatoes, chopped

1 tablespoon chopped red pepper

1 tablespoon chopped green pepper

2–3 fresh green chillies, chopped

salt to taste

◆

1. Strain the sweetcorn. Reserve the liquid and make it up to 3½fl oz (100ml) with water if necessary.

2. Heat the oil in a balti pan, wok or large frying pan and stir-fry the seeds for 10 seconds. Add the garlic and ginger and continue stir-frying for about a minute. Add the curry powder and garam masala and stir-fry for a further minute.

3. Now add the onion flakes, stirring briskly until they absorb the oil and start sizzling. Add the sweetcorn liquid/water and bring the pan to a simmer.

4. Add the sweetcorn to the pan with the mushrooms and all the other ingredients except the salt. Simmer gently for 2–3 minutes, then add salt to taste.

Balti Chicken, Broccoli, Lentils and Peas

—— SERVES 2 as a main course ——

Here is a typical combination of balti ingredients. The mixture should not only include different tastes, it should also include different shapes, colours and textures. To achieve speed, thaw the frozen broccoli and peas in the microwave and use leftover lentils to make Quick Tasty Dhal, page 84. If you don't have lentils, omit them altogether, but increase the peas and broccoli. If you don't have a microwave, remember to take the frozen vegetables out of the freezer ahead of time.

◆

½ lb (225g) boned chicken breasts, skinned

3oz (75g) frozen broccoli

2oz (50g) frozen peas

4 tablespoons vegetable or butter ghee or vegetable oil

½ teaspoon white cummin seeds

½ teaspoon fennel seeds

¼ teaspoon green cardamom seeds

2 teaspoons bottled minced garlic

1 teaspoon bottled minced ginger

1 tablespoon home-made curry powder (see page 7)

1 tablespoon garam masala (see page 6)

6 tablespoons dried onion flakes

3fl oz (75ml) tomato juice

2fl oz (50ml) red wine (optional)

1 tablespoon chopped red pepper

1 fresh green chilli, chopped; use more if you wish

1 teaspoon dried fenugreek leaves

2 tablespoons Greek yoghurt

1 tablespoon chopped fresh green coriander leaves

3–4 tablespoons cooked lentils (Quick Tasty Dhal, see page 84)

salt to taste

whole fresh coriander leaves

◆

1. Cut the chicken into bite-sized (about 1¼ inch/3.25cm) pieces. Soften the broccoli and peas in the microwave.

2. Heat half the ghee or oil in a balti pan, wok or large frying pan. Stir-fry the seeds for 20 seconds. Add the garlic and ginger and continue to stir-fry for 30 seconds more. Add the remaining ghee or oil and the curry powder and garam masala.

3. Add the onion flakes and stir-fry briskly. They will absorb the oil quickly and could start burning. Before they do, add the tomato juice, and the red wine if using or 2fl oz (50ml) water. Bring to a simmer and add the chicken, pepper, chilli and fenugreek leaves.

4. Keep on stir-frying for about 10 minutes, then add the yoghurt, fresh coriander, broccoli, peas and lentils.

5. Continue stir-frying until the chicken is cooked right through (about another 5 minutes) and watch the liquid balance. The mixture should not be dry nor should it be swamped; you will probably need to add a tablespoon of water from time to time.

6. Add salt to taste, garnish with whole coriander leaves and serve.

Balti Mince, Prawns, Chickpeas and Spinach

—— SERVES 2 as a main course ——

Compare this combination with that in the previous recipe. Again it gives a great range of contrasts. Mince is a great curry subject as it is almost indestructible. It requires slightly longer cooking than most of the recipes in this book, so I recommend a slowish cook on the stove top. If you don't fancy the prawns, omit them and increase the mince quantity.

2 tablespoons vegetable oil
½ lb (225g) minced lean beef, lamb or pork
2 tablespoons butter ghee
4oz (110g) canned chickpeas, drained and their liquid reserved (see Step 1)
4 tablespoons white cummin seeds
½ teaspoon fennel seeds
¼ teaspoon green cardamom seeds
2 teaspoons bottled minced garlic
1 teaspoon bottled minced ginger
1 tablespoon home-made curry powder (see page 7)
1 tablespoon garam masala (see page 6)

6 tablespoons dried onion flakes
3fl oz (75ml) tomato juice
2fl oz (50ml) red wine (optional)
2oz (50g) peeled cooked prawns
1 tablespoon chopped red pepper
1 fresh green chilli, chopped (optional); use more if you wish
1 teaspoon dried fenugreek leaves
10–12 spinach leaves, chopped
2 tablespoons Greek yoghurt
1 tablespoon chopped fresh green coriander leaves
salt to taste

1. Heat the oil in a saucepan. Add the mince and cook for about 20 minutes on medium heat, stirring occasionally. If it is a little dry, put the reserved chickpea liquid in spoonful by spoonful.

2. After about 15 minutes heat half the ghee or oil in a balti pan, wok or large frying pan. Stir-fry the seeds for 20 seconds. Add the garlic and ginger and continue to stir-fry for 30 seconds more. Add the remaining ghee or oil and the curry powder and garam masala.

3. Add the onion flakes and stir-fry briskly. They will absorb the oil quickly and could start burning. Before they do, add the tomato

juice, and the red wine if using or 2fl oz (50ml) water. Bring to a simmer and add the prawns, pepper, chilli if using and fenugreek leaves.

4. Keep on stir-frying for about 5 minutes, then add the chickpeas, spinach, yoghurt and fresh coriander.

5. Continue stir-frying until the mince is the tenderness you like (at least another 5 minutes) and watch the liquid balance. The mixture should not be dry nor should it be swamped; you will probably need to add a tablespoon of water from time to time.

6. Add salt to taste and serve.

CHAPTER 5

MEAT CURRIES

The problem with cooking meat is that it takes at least 45 minutes to go from raw to tender. One answer if you are aiming to cook a meat curry from scratch in under half an hour is to cut the meat into much smaller pieces than the traditional 1¼–1½ inch (3.25–3.75cm) cubes. I use ½ inch (1.25cm) pieces in my recipes and it works well. The other solution is to cut the meat into thin slices, Chinese stir-fry style, which cook even faster. This is recommended when you want the fastest possible results. Use only best quality lean meat. It tastes better and requires the least preparation time because there is minimal unwanted matter (gristle, fat, membranes, etc.) to trim off and discard.

These eight recipes give you a variety of meats in a variety of modes.

Sheek Kebab – Burger Style

—— SERVES 2 as a snack (makes 4 kebabs) ——

The traditional sheek kebab is skewered and cooked in a clay oven. The trick in making the kebab hold its shape is to use meat which you have ground down in a food processor or hand mincer. (Bought mince will not hold together.) As this is messy, you could make a large quantity of fully spiced, ground kebab meat using, say 4lb (1.8kg), and freeze it in batches. Serve the kebabs like burgers, in buns, with salad and chutney.

1lb (450g) lean stewing steak, divested of all fat, gristle, etc.

2–3 cloves garlic, chopped

1 tablespoon chopped fresh mint

2 tablespoons chopped fresh green coriander leaves

4 tablespoons dried onion flakes, crumbled

2 teaspoons tandoori curry powder (see page 8)

1 teaspoon garam masala (see page 6)

1 teaspoon white cummin seeds

1–2 fresh green chillies, chopped (optional)

½ teaspoon salt

3 tablespoons butter ghee

---

1. Cut the meat into small pieces.

2. Combine all the ingredients except the ghee, divide them into 3 or 4 batches of roughly equal amounts and put them through the food processor.

3. Now, using your hands, work them together until well blended.

4. Divide the mixture into 4 and mould into burger or rissole shapes.

5. Heat the ghee in a large frying pan. Fry the kebabs on medium heat for at least 5 minutes a side, or longer, depending on how rare or well done you want them.

Non-skewer Shashlik

—— SERVES 2 ——

This is an ancient Middle Eastern favourite. Chunks of marinated meat interspersed with onion and pepper are skewered and grilled. For time's sake I have dispensed with the marinade and the grill. The trick is to cut thin strips of steak (about 1½ × 1 × ¼ inch/3.25 × 2.5cm × 6mm). If you chill the meat (almost freeze it) before cutting it will slice easily. All the ingredients are then rapidly stir-fired. If you have the time you could thread them on to bamboo skewers after cooking. Note the last ingredient – the secret weapon that adds an interesting kick. Serve on a bed of rice with salad, lemon wedges and chutneys.

10oz (300g) thick frying or fillet steak
½ red pepper, cored and deseeded
½ green pepper, cored and deseeded
1 small onion
2 tablespoons vegetable oil
1 teaspoon bottled minced garlic
1 teaspoon bottled minced ginger

1 tablespoon home-made curry powder (see page 7)
2 fresh red chillies (optional)
salt to taste
1 teaspoon garam masala (see page 6)
4 tablespoons dry sherry

---

1. Cut the meat into 3.25 × 2.5 cm × 6 mm (1½ × 1 x ¼ inch) slices.

2. Cut the peppers and onion into similar shapes to the meat.

3. Heat the oil in a wok or karahi. Stir-fry the garlic and ginger for 20 seconds. Add the curry powder and a tablespoon of water and stir-fry for about one minute.

4. Add the meat, peppers, onion and chillies if using and stir-fry briskly for 3–4 minutes.

5. Add salt to taste and the garam masala and sherry and continue to stir-fry until the meat is as tender as you want it to be (another 1–5 minutes).

Sag Gosht

—— SERVES 2 ——

Sag means spinach and *gosht* means meat. This dish is from the Punjab – the north-west corner of the sub-continent, now straddled by Pakistan and India. Spinach and meat go together, for me, like peaches and cream or curry and rice! Here's a quick version. Serve it indeed with rice or, as the Punjabis do, with naan bread – and add a salad, lemon wedges and chutneys.

◆

12oz (350g) lean stewing steak, divested of all fat, gristle, etc.

4 tablespoons vegetable or butter ghee

3 teaspoons bottled minced garlic

1 teaspoon bottled minced ginger

1 tablespoon home-made curry powder (see page 7)

4oz (110g) spring onions (leaves and bulbs), chopped

5fl oz (150ml) onion soup, stock or water

1 tablespoon tomato purée

1 tablespoon tomato ketchup

1 teaspoon dried fenugreek leaves

6oz (175g) spinach leaves, chopped

1 teaspoon bottled vinegared mint

1 tablespoon chopped fresh green coriander leaves

2 teaspoons garam masala (see page 6)

salt to taste

SPICES

1 teaspoon white cummin seeds

½ teaspoon fennel seeds

2–3 green cardamoms

2–3 bay leaves

◆

1. Cut the meat into small cubes (about ½ inch/1.3cm).

2. Heat the ghee in a wok or karahi. Stir-fry the **spices** for 20 seconds. Add the garlic and ginger and continue to stir-fry for 30 seconds more. Add the curry powder and briskly stir-fry it in, then add a tablespoon or two of water.

3. Add the meat and spring onions, and stir-fry for about 5 minutes. Control the liquid content by adding water as above. There should be just enough liquid to achieve a simmer without sticking.

4. Add the soup, stock or water, the tomato purée, ketchup and fenugreek leaves. Simmer for another 5 minutes, stirring as necessary.

5. Add the spinach leaves, mint, fresh coriander and garam masala and simmer and stir until the meat is as tender as you want – a minimum of 5 minutes. Add salt to taste.

Grilled Spicy Ribs

—— SERVES 2 ——

Ribs or chops are not a traditional Indian cut of meat. However, they respond very well to spicy treatment, as in Grilled Tandoori Chops (see page 26). The spices are different in this recipe. Serve the ribs with rice and chutneys.

◆

4 lamb or pork ribs, total weight 1lb (450g) on the bone
6 tablespoons soya or sunflower oil
1 teaspoon ground coriander
1 teaspoon ground white cummin
½ teaspoon chilli powder
2 teaspoons home-made curry powder (see page 7)

1 teaspoon bottled vinegared mint
2 teaspoons bottled minced coriander
½ teaspoon salt

GARNISH
snipped chives

◆

1. Preheat the grill to medium, line the grill tray with foil and put the rack over it.

2. Cut small slashes into the ribs with a sharp knife.

3. Mix all the remaining ingredients together in a large non-metallic bowl.

4. Coat the ribs throughly with the mixture, then put them on the grill rack. Place the tray midway from the heat. Grill the ribs for 5 minutes.

5. Turn the ribs over and baste them with any remaining mixture. Grill for another 5 minutes.

6. Depending on your grill's efficiency, the ribs should now be cooked. Check by cutting into one. If necessary, continue grilling until the ribs are cooked.

7. Pour over spare juices, if any, and garnish with the chives.

Spicy Escalope of Veal or Pork

—— **SERVES 2** ——

Both these light, pale meats are simply divine beaten and coated with breadcrumbs. Here the coating has a spicy flavour. Eat this quickly cooked and very satisfying dish with a salad and Plain Boiled Rice (see page 99) into which you have stirred a knob or two of unsalted butter and some chilli powder, or with the Spicy Spaghetti or Noodles on page 12 (served hot).

---

2 escalopes of veal or pork, each weighing about 6oz (175g)
2 large eggs
2 teaspoons garam masala (see page 6)
2 teaspoons finely chopped fresh green coriander leaves

1 teaspoon snipped chives
1 fresh red chilli, finely chopped
½ teaspoon salt
2oz (50g) breadcrumbs
3 tablespoons butter

---

1. Beat the escalopes until thin, if necessary, and dry them with kitchen paper.

2. Beat the eggs in a bowl with all the remaining ingredients except the breadcrumbs and butter.

3. Coat the escalopes with the egg mixture, then dab them into the breadcrumbs. Press the breadcrumbs firmly on to the escalopes.

4. Heat the butter in a large frying pan, then fry the escalopes for 4–6 minutes a side. (The exact timing will depend on the heat and the thickness of the escalopes).

Spicy Chilli and Pepper Steak

—— SERVES 2 ——

Here's an advance on the highly popular pepper steak. Chillies and spices are incorporated into the steak, which is then pan-fried for 3 minutes a side for rare, 4–6 minutes a side for medium and 6–10 minutes a side for well done. The times in this recipe are for fillet steak about 1¼ inch (3.25cm) thick. Other steak cuts such as rump or sirloin may take longer. Serve with a salad or, if you want something more substantial, with rice and a mix-in sauce from Chapter 9.

---

2 fillet steaks, each weighing about
  6oz (175g)
2 tablespoons oil

COATING
½ teaspoon black peppercorns, crushed
½ teaspoon white cummin seeds,
  roasted (see page 4)
⅓ teaspoon green peppercorns in
  brine, crushed

⅓ teaspoon coriander seeds, roasted
  (see page 4) then crushed
1 tablespoon finely chopped fresh
  green coriander leaves
1 fresh green chilli, finely chopped
1 teaspoon garam masala (see page 6)
⅓ teaspoon turmeric

---

1. Mix all the coating ingredients together in a bowl.

2. Dab both sides of the steaks into the mixture.

3. Heat the oil in a frying pan. Fry the steaks for between 3 minutes and 10 minutes a side (see above). The longer the cooking time, the more the coating will get burned. This can be minimized by adding a teaspoon of water from time to time.

Meat Curry (Stir-fried)

—— SERVES 2 ——

As explained on page 48, cooking a fully fledged meat curry really does need an hour in a casserole. Two other quick, stir-fried meat curries are Instant Meat Tikka (see page 25) and Balti Meat (see page 38). Here is another quick method. It was developed by the British in India as a way to use up, at dinner-time, joints left over from lunch. They called it jal-frezi (dry-fry). This now means something different in restaurants, but this is the original 'dry-fry' of leftover cooked meat. Note the use of prawn bal-lichow pickle which adds a magical (unidentifiable) flavour to the dish.

◆

10oz (300g) leftover cold meat, divested of all fat, gristle, etc.
2 tablespoons butter ghee
2 teaspoons bottled minced garlic
1 tablespoon home-made curry powder (see page 7)
3fl oz (75ml) tomato juice
6oz (110g) dried onion flakes
2 tablespoons butter
1 tablespoon prawn ballichow (optional)
2oz (50 g) carrot, sliced
1 tablespoon chopped red pepper
1 tablespoon chopped green pepper

1–2 fresh green chillies, chopped
1 teaspoon bottled minced coriander
2–3 spring onions (leaves and bulbs), chopped
2fl oz (50ml) single cream
1–2 teaspoons garam masala
salt to taste

SPICES
1 teaspoon white cummin seeds
½ teaspoon black mustard seed
½ teaspoon sesame seeds
½ teaspoon turmeric
¼ teaspoon chilli powder

◆

1. Cut the cold meat into bite-sized pieces.

2. Heat the ghee in a wok or karahi. Stir-fry the **spices** for 20 seconds, then add the garlic and stir-fry for a further 20 seconds. Add the curry powder and stir-fry for another 30 seconds. Then add 2–3 tablespoons of the tomato juice.

3. Now add the onion flakes and stir-fry briskly for 30 seconds more. Add the rest of the tomato juice and the butter. When sizzling, add the prawn ballichow if using, carrot, peppers, chilli, minced coriander and spring onions.

4. Stir-fry for about 4 minutes, then add the cream, meat and garam masala and simmer for another 5 minutes. Add salt to taste and serve.

Mince Curry (Keema) with Red Kidney Beans

—— SERVES 2 ——

The Balti Mince, Prawns, Chickpeas and Spinach on page 46 is quite different from this curry which comes originally from Kashmir and uses ginger (plenty of it), chillies (as many as you dare) and red kidney beans which are canned to save time. Serve with rice or bread.

◆

2 tablespoons vegetable oil
10oz (300g) minced beef, lamb or pork
2 tablespoons butter or vegetable ghee
2 teaspoons bottled minced garlic
1oz (25g) fresh ginger, shredded or finely chopped
1–4 fresh red chillies, sliced
3oz (75g) spring onions (leaves and bulbs), chopped
3–4 canned plum tomatoes

1 tablespoon tomato ketchup
3oz (75g) canned red kidney beans
1 tablespoon chopped fresh coriander
salt to taste

SPICES
2 teaspoons garam masala
1 teaspoon ground coriander
½ teaspoon ground cummin
½ teaspoon chilli powder (or more)

◆

1. Heat the oil in a saucepan. Add the mince and cook for about 20 minutes on medium heat, stirring occasionally. If it needs a little liquid, add water spoonful by spoonful.

2. After about 15 minutes heat the ghee in a wok, karahi or large frying pan. Stir-fry the **spices** for 30 seconds. Add the garlic and continue stir-frying for 30 seconds. Add the ginger, chillies and spring onions and continue stir-frying for a further minute.

3. Transfer the mince to the wok, mixing well. Add the tomatoes and ketchup, and simmer for about another 5 minutes.

4. Strain the kidney beans and rinse them. Then add them to the wok with the fresh coriander. Cook for another 5 minutes, adding a little water if necessary. Add salt to taste.

CHAPTER 6

POULTRY CURRIES

Chicken is a gift for the rapid curry cook. It takes less than 15 minutes to cook, even in quite large chunks. In the recipes here 1½ inch (3.75cm) pieces are the norm. It is essential that the chicken pieces are cooked right through and that this is done at a high temperature. Cut the largest chunk of chicken in half in the pan to check that there is no raw, uncooked meat in the centre. Poultry in curry dishes is always skinned.

Murgh Kebab – Burger Style

—— SERVES 2 as a snack (makes 4 kebabs) ——

Sheek Kebab – Burger Style, the meat equivalent of this recipe, is on page 49. This one uses chicken leg meat (or the cheaper turkey leg meat) which is ground in a food processor. Chicken is a very welcome alternative to red meat in this burger-style kebab. Serve in buns like burgers, with salad and chutneys.

◆

1 lb (450g) boned chicken or turkey leg meat, skinned

2–3 cloves garlic, chopped

1 tablespoon chopped fresh mint

2 tablespoons chopped fresh green coriander

4 tablespoons dried onion flakes, crumbled

2 teaspoons tandoori curry powder (see page 8)

1 teaspoon garam masala (see page 6)

1 teaspoon white cummin seeds

1–2 fresh green chillies, chopped (optional)

½ teaspoon salt

3 tablespoons butter ghee

◆

1. Cut the chicken into 1½ inch (3.75cm) pieces.

2. Combine all the ingredients except the ghee, divide them into 3 or 4 batches of roughly equal amounts and put them through the food processor.

3. Now, using your hands, mix them together until well blended.

4. Divide the mixture into 4 and mould into burger or rissole shapes.

5. Heat the ghee in a large frying pan. Fry the kebabs on medium heat for at least 5 minutes a side, or longer, depending on how rare or well done you want them.

Chile-and-Pepper Steak **(page 54)** served with Bombay Potatoes **(page 81)** and Kashmiri Salad **(page 15)**.

Ground Turkey Curry **(page 65)** served with Kitchri **(page 103)** and Spiced Shredded Vegetable Salad **(page 14)**.

Corn-and-Mushroom Stir-Fry **(page 43)** served with Madrasi Sambar **(page 82)** and White Coconut Raita **(page 109)**.

Balti Chicken, Brocholi, Lentils, and Peas **(page 44)** served with Curry
Yellow Raita **(page 109)**.

Goan Shrimp Curry **(page 71)** served with Quick Tasty Dhal **(page 84)** and Popadoms **(page 18)**.

Mushroom Bhaji **(page 78)** served with Pea Pullao Rice **(page 100)** and Muglai Sauce **(page 92)**.

Chicken Tikka Masala **(page 30)** on Fried Pullao Rice **(page100)** served with Aloo Ghobi Sag **(page 80)** and an Indian bread.

Stir-Fried Shashlik **(page 50)** served with Plain Boiled Rice **(page 99)** and Red Chile Chutney **(page 111)**.

Non-Skewer Hasina

—— SERVES 2 as a snack (makes 4 kebabs) ——

This recipe, like Non-skewer Shaslik (see page 50), originated in the Middle East. It uses chicken and it too should have a long marination before being slid on to skewers alternately with slices of onion and pepper. Again, I have dispensed with the marinade, the clay oven and the skewers, although you could put the hasinas on bamboo skewers if you feel inclined. Serve on a bed of rice together with salad, lemon wedges and chutneys.

◆

10oz (300g) boned chicken breasts, skinned
½ red pepper, cored and deseeded
½ green pepper, cored and deseeded
1 small onion
2 tablespoons vegetable oil
1 teaspoon bottled minced garlic
1 teaspoon bottled minced ginger
1 tablespoon home-made curry powder (see page 7)
2 fresh red chillies (optional)
1 teaspoon garam masala (see page 6)
4 tablespoons dry sherry
salt to taste

◆

1. Cut the chicken into 1 inch (2.5cm) cubes.

2. Cut the peppers and onion into 1 inch (2.5cm) squares

3. Heat the oil in a wok or karahi. Stir-fry the garlic and ginger for 20 seconds. Add the curry powder and a tablespoon of water and stir-fry for about one minute.

4. Add the chicken and stir-fry briskly for 6–8 minutes.

5. Add the onion, peppers, chillies, garam masala and sherry, and continue to stir-fry until the chicken is as tender as you want it (another 6–10 minutes). Add salt to taste.

Chicken Jalfrezi

—— **SERVES 2** ——

As I explained on page 55, *jal-frezi* (meaning dry-fry) was one of the ways in which the Raj used up leftovers. And the remains of cold roast chicken would not escape these attentions. Nowadays this dish has come to mean a stir-fry of fresh ingredients, in this case chicken, with lovely, yellow-golden curry spices and herbs and a little chilli. For those who like more chilli, the recipe on page 63 is just for you. Serve with plain rice and chutneys.

10oz (300g) boned chicken breasts, skinned

3 tablespoons butter ghee

1 teaspoon white cummin seeds

1 teaspoon sesame seeds

½ teaspoon turmeric

2–4 cloves garlic, chopped

1 inch (2.5cm) cube fresh ginger, chopped

1 tablespoon home-made curry powder (see page 7)

4 tablespoons dried onion flakes

1 tablespoon chopped red pepper

1–2 fresh green chillies, chopped

2–3 tomatoes, quartered

1oz (25g) creamed coconut, chopped

1 teaspoon bottled minced coriander

1 tablespoon brinjal (aubergine) pickle, chopped

2 teaspoons chopped fresh green coriander leaves, and/or

2 teaspoons chopped fresh mint leaves

1 teaspoon garam masala

salt to taste

---

1. Cut the chicken breasts into generous bite-sized pieces.

2. Heat the ghee in a wok or karahi. Stir-fry the seeds and turmeric for 20 seconds. Add the garlic and ginger and continue stir-frying for 30 seconds more. Add the curry powder and 1–2 tablespoons water, and stir-fry for another minute.

3. Add the chicken pieces, onion flakes, pepper and chilli and stir-fry for 3–4 minutes, adding spoonfuls of water as needed to keep things mobile.

4. Lower the heat, add the tomatoes, creamed coconut, minced coriander and brinjal pickle and cook for about 10 minutes, stirring occasionally and adding water as needed.

5. Add the fresh coriander and/or mint, garam masala and salt to taste.

Jeera Chicken

—— **SERVES 2** ——

As far as I can ascertain this recipe developed amongst the Indo-Asian populations of Kenya and Uanda. You will encounter it at a few restaurants run by African Asians, but it is rare to find. Which is a pity. If you happen to adore the earthy, musky, savoury taste of jeera (cummin) you'll enjoy this recipe. It uses jeera in no less than three ways: whole fried seeds, ground fried cummin and roasted seeds for garnish.

10oz (300g) boned chicken breasts, skinned
3 tablespoons butter ghee
2 teaspoons white cummin seeds
1 teaspoon sesame seeds
2 teaspoons ground cummin
2–4 cloves garlic, chopped
1 inch (2.5cm) cube fresh ginger, chopped
1 teaspoon home-made curry powder (see page 7)
4 tablespoons dried onion flakes
1 tablespoon chopped red pepper
1–2 fresh red chillies, chopped

2–3 tomatoes, quartered
1oz (25g) creamed coconut, chopped
1 tablespoon mango chutney, chopped
1 tablespoon brinjal (aubergine) pickle
1 tablespoon chopped fresh green coriander leaves
2 teaspoons garam masala (see page 6)
salt to taste

GARNISH
2 teaspoons white cummin seeds, roasted (see page 4)

---

1. Cut the chicken breasts into generous bite-sized pieces.

2. Heat the ghee in a wok or karahi. Stir-fry the seeds and ground cummin for 20 seconds. Add the garlic and ginger and continue stir-frying for 30 seconds more. Add the curry powder and continue to stir-fry for a further minute.

3. Add the chicken pieces, onion flakes, pepper and chilli and stir-fry for 3–4 minutes, adding spoonfuls of water as needed.

4. Lower the heat, add the tomatoes, creamed coconut, mango chutney and brinjal pickle, and cook for about 10 minutes, stirring occasionally and adding water as needed.

5. Add the fresh coriander, garam masala and salt to taste. Garnish with the roasted cummin seeds.

Butter Chicken

—— SERVES 2 ——

This rich dish goes under the name Makhani Chicken in India, where it uses white buffalo butter. I've substituted ordinary butter and used minimal spicing. To prevent swamping its unique caramelized flavours, I recommend that you serve it with Plain Boiled Rice (see page 99) and, if you feel it needs more, maybe Quick Tasty Dhal (see page 84).

10oz (300g) boned chicken breasts, skinned

2 tablespoons butter ghee

1 tablespoon Bengali five spice mixture (see page 8)

2 teaspoons paprika

½ teaspoon chilli powder

2–4 cloves, garlic, chopped

2–3 tablespoons butter

1 teaspoon tandoori curry powder (see page 8)

4 tablespoons dried onion flakes

2 tablespoons chopped red pepper

1 fresh red chilli, chopped

3–4 tomatoes, quartered

1 tablespoon tomato purée

1 tablespoon mango chutney, chopped

2 teaspoons chopped fresh green coriander leaves

2 teaspoons chopped fresh basil leaves

1 teaspoon garam masala (see page 6)

salt to taste

---

1. Cut the chicken breasts into generous bite-sized pieces.

2. Heat the ghee in a wok or karahi. Stir-fry the five spice mixture, paprika and chilli powder for 20 seconds. Add the garlic and stir-fry for 30 seconds more. Now add the butter and curry powder.

3. Add the chicken pieces, onion flakes, pepper and chilli and stir-fry for 3–4 minutes, adding spoonfuls of water as needed to keep things mobile.

4. Lower the heat, add the tomatoes, tomato purée and mango chutney and cook for about 10 minutes, stirring occasionally and adding water as needed.

5. Add the fresh coriander, basil, garam masala and salt to taste.

Chilli Chicken

—— SERVES 2 ——

There are some people to whom this recipe is IT! They will turn to the index, look up 'chilli' and drool over this page. Scientists have written pages and pages explaining why people enjoy chilli. And if you'd like to know, and if you like chillies, read my book *Curry Club 250 Hot and Spicy Dishes* published by Piatkus. But save that for later, there's no time now! Because in 20 minutes you could be gobbling down this uncompromisingly chilli-hot dish.

10oz (300g) boned chicken breasts or legs, skinned
3 tablespoons vegetable oil
1 teaspoon white cummin seeds
½ teaspoon coriander seeds
½ teaspoon black mustard seeds
1 teaspoon extra-hot chilli powder
1 tablespoon bottled minced garlic
1 tablespoon home-made curry powder (page 7)
4 tablespoons dried onion flakes

1 tablespoon red pepper, chopped
2–4 fresh green chillies, chopped
2–3 canned tomatoes, chopped
1oz (25g) creamed coconut, chopped
1 teaspoon bottled vinegared mint
1–2 tablespoons chilli pickle, chopped
1 tablespoon chopped fresh green coriander leaves
2 tablespoons chopped fresh mint
1 teaspoon garam masala (see page 6)
salt to taste

---

1. Cut the chicken into generous bite-sized pieces.

2. Heat the oil in a wok or karahi. Stir-fry the seeds and chilli powder for 20 seconds. Add the garlic and continue stir-frying for 30 seconds more. Add the curry powder and 1–2 tablespoons water and stir-fry for another minute.

3. Add the chicken pieces, onion flakes, pepper and chillies and stir-fry for 3–4 minutes, adding spoonfuls of water as needed to keep things mobile.

4. Lower the heat, add the tomatoes, creamed coconut, bottled mint and chilli pickle and cook for about 10 minutes, stirring occasionally and adding water as needed.

5. Add the fresh coriander, mint, garam masala and salt to taste.

Chicken Dopiaza

—— SERVES 2 ——

Do means two, piaza means onion and this recipe uses a lot of onions in four different ways. In fact, my interpretation uses ordinary onions in the early stages, then shallots and finally spring onions. To ring the changes from previous recipes I have used chicken drumsticks, the part of the leg below the thigh. I have also used used canned French onion soup as stock, so the result is really oniony – but totally delicious. Use two decent-sized drumsticks per person; with the nice, juicy bones to suck on that will be ample. This dish is best casseroled in the oven, so it takes longer than most of the other recipes in this chapter. It will be lovely and runny when cooked and is best served in bowls. It can, of course, be cooked then chilled or frozen, just waiting to be re-heated when needed.

---

2 tablespoons sunflower oil

1 × 2inch (5cm) piece cassia bark

1 star anise

2 brown cardamoms

4–6 cloves

1 tablespoon home-made curry powder (see page 7)

4oz (100g) onions, chopped

4 small pickling onions or shallots, peeled and halved

2–3 bay leaves

200ml (7fl oz) canned onion soup

4 skinned chicken drumsticks, each weighing about 4–4½oz (100–120g)

2–3 spring onions, (leaves and bulbs), cut into strips, lengthways

1 dried red chilli, chopped; use more if you wish

1½ teaspoons garam masala (see page 6)

salt to taste

---

1. Preheat the oven to 375°F/190°C/Gas Mark 5.

2. Heat the oil in a lidded casserole dish and fry the cassia bark, star anise, cardamoms and cloves for 10 seconds.

3. Add the curry powder and stir-fry for 30 seconds. Now add the chopped onion and stir-fry on lowish heat for 5 minutes.

4. Next add the pickling onions, bay leaves, onion soup and drumsticks. Keep on a high heat until simmering, then transfer to the oven.

5. After 15 minutes add the spring onions, red chilli and garam masala. Give it 15 more minutes in the oven, making 30 minutes' oven time in all. Check that the chicken is cooked through, add salt and serve.

Minced Chicken or Turkey Curry

—— **SERVES 2** ——

Use skinned chicken or turkey leg meat for this and, unless you really have neither the time nor the energy, mince your own. You will have a superb ingredient which stir-fries to completion in around 12 minutes. As that's quicker than it takes to prepare rice (unless you have some already cooked in the fridge), you could serve it with bread and a salad.

◆

3 tablespoons butter ghee
1 teaspoon white cummin seeds
½ teaspoon coriander seeds
½ teaspoon fennel seeds
⅓ teaspoon lovage seeds (optional)
⅓ teaspoon green cardamom seeds
1 teaspoon bottled minced garlic
2 teaspoons home-made curry powder (see page 7)
9oz (225g) skinless chicken or turkey, leg or breast, minced
4oz (110g) spring onions (leaves and bulbs), chopped
2 tablespoons chopped green pepper
1–2 fresh red chillies, chopped
3–4 cherry tomatoes, quartered
5fl oz (150ml) canned cream of mushroom soup
8–10 fresh button mushrooms, quartered
1 teaspoon prepared English mustard
1 teaspoon horseradish sauce
1 teaspoon bottled minced coriander
1 tablespoon chopped fresh green coriander leaves
1 teaspoon garam masala (see page 6)
salt to taste

◆

1. Heat the ghee in a wok or karahi. Stir-fry the seeds for 20 seconds. Add the garlic and continue to stir-fry for 30 seconds more. Add the curry powder and stir in well. After a few seconds' cooking add 1–2 tablespoons of water to prevent burning.

2. Add the mince and stir for a couple of minutes, then add the spring onions, pepper, chilli and tomato and mix in well. When sizzling, start adding the soup a tablespoon at a time over a 5-minute period so that it blends with and cooks in the other ingredients rather than swamping them.

3. The contents of the wok should by now be quite creamy in texture, but sizzling nicely. Add all the remaining ingredients except the salt and simmer for another 5 minutes. Add salt to taste and serve.

CHAPTER 7

◆

FISH AND SEAFOOD CURRIES

Some of the sub-continent's best dishes are, in my view, her fish and shellfish curries. I wish we encountered more of them in restaurants. The seven recipes here all quite different in character. Four of them, in particular, are authentic recipes from India and Bangladesh. It is worth making the effort to track down the huge tiger prawns for Jeera Tiger Prawns (see page 67). Bangladeshi Lobster and Shrimp Jal-frezi (see page 69) is expensive, but worth having on that special occasion As for Scampi Creamy Kofta (see page 68) – it's my invention but it's very tasty and, as with all the recipes in this chapter, very quick to cook.

Jeera Tiger Prawns

—— SERVES 2 ——

You will need those gigantic prawns which weigh up to 150g (6oz) without their heads. You know the ones: they serve them in Indian restaurants. For some reason they are not readily available, particularly, it seems, in supermarkets. You can obtain them frozen but you may have to order them from a good fishmonger. Native to the Bay of Bengal, they are called tiger prawns because of the black stripes that adorn their backs. Buy uncooked frozen tiger prawns without heads but with shells and tails. They are unpeeled and as less water is frozen with them you get more prawn for your money. Allow 24 hours in a covered bowl in the fridge for them to thaw. This recipe maximizes their flavour and fabulous meaty texture with minimal spicing. Serve with lime wedges and Indian bread.

---

4 headless, unpeeled Bengal tiger
   prawns, each weighing over 100g
   (4oz)
juice of 2 limes
1 tablespoon butter ghee
1 tablespoon butter
2 teaspoons white cummin seeds
½ teaspoon turmeric
1 teaspoon home-made curry powder
   (see page 7)

2 cloves garlic, finely chopped
2–3 spring onions (leaves and bulbs),
   finely chopped
salt to taste

GARNISH
snipped chives
desiccated coconut
chilli powder

---

1. When the prawns are fully thawed remove the shell, legs and tail. Cut a slit down the back and pull out the vein. Wash the prawns, pat them dry with kitchen paper, then massage them with the lime juice.

2. Heat the ghee and butter in a wok or karahi. Stir-fry the cummin seeds for 20 seconds. Add the turmeric and curry powder and stir-fry for 20 seconds. Add the garlic and spring onions.

3. Stir-fry the mixture for 2–3 minutes. Then add the prawns. Stir-fry for about 12 minutes, aiming to maintain a gentle sizzle without burning the spices. Add tiny quantities of water to prevent sticking.

4. When the prawns are ready their centres should be an even bright white. Cut one in half to check.

5. Salt to taste, garnish with the chives, coconut and chilli and serve.

Scampi Creamy Kofta

—— SERVES 2 ——

I happen to adore breaded scampi. They are one of life's great convenience foods. I also happen to adore immersing them in a rich curry sauce. This merging of East and West creates what I call the ultra-quick Scampi Kofta. The amounts of soup and cream or milk will vary according to the creaminess or thickness of the soup. Please be sure to get whole (real) scampi, not the reprocessed or re-formed (cheap) ones which contain I know what not, and taste of nothing.

◆

4 tablespoons butter or vegetable ghee
1 teaspoon sesame seeds
½ teaspoon lovage seeds
½ teaspoon wild onion seeds
½ teaspoon turmeric
2 teaspoons bottled minced garlic
3oz (75g) spring onions (bulbs and leaves), chopped
2 teaspoons home-made curry powder (see page 7)
1 teaspoon tandoori curry powder (see page 8)

4–6fl oz (110–175ml) canned or carton vichyssoise or leek and potato soup
1 fresh green chilli, sliced (optional)
2–3 tomatoes, quartered
1 tablespoon prawn ballichow
½ teaspoon bottled minced coriander
single cream or milk (see above)
3 tablespoons vegetable oil
1 lb (500g) frozen breaded scampi
salt to taste

◆

1. Heat the ghee in a wok or karahi. Stir-fry the seeds for 10 seconds. Add the turmeric and stir-fry for 10 more seconds. Now add the garlic and stir-fry for 30 seconds. Add the spring onions and continue for a couple of minutes, then add the curry powders.

2. Now add the soup, a spoonful at a time over a 3-minute period to keep the sizzle going and to avoid swamping the mixture.

3. Add the chilli, tomatoes, prawn ballichow, coriander and enough cream or milk to simmer gently without sticking as the scampi cook.

4. Heat the oil in a flat frying pan. Introduce the frozen scampi to the pan in threes and fours over a couple of minutes, stir-frying all the

Lobster and Shrimp Jalfrezi

—— **SERVES 2** ——

Occasionally we all want to cook something special, to mark a birthday or anniversary – or just to be different. And as such dates often fall on work days, here is a plush recipe which only takes minutes to cook. Serve with rice like Chicken Tikka Pullao (see page 104) and – since money is no object – buy a dozen red roses and break out the pink champagne.

◆

4oz (110g) potted shrimps in butter

2–3 tablespoons butter or vegetable ghee

½ teaspoon fennel seeds

½ teaspoon sesame seeds

½ teaspoon white poppy seeds

⅓ teaspoon wild onion seeds

⅓ teaspoon turmeric

2–3 cloves garlic, chopped

1 tablespoon home-made curry powder (see page 7)

3fl oz (75ml) milk

4 tablespoons fried dried onion flakes

½ lb (225g) cooked lobster meat

3fl oz (75ml) single cream

1 tablespoon prawn ballichow

1 tablespoon chopped fresh green coriander leaves

2 teaspoons ground almonds

1 teaspoon garam masala (see page 6)

salt to taste

◆

1. Put the shrimps with their butter topping into a pan to melt down the butter. Strain the butter off into a wok or karahi, keeping the shrimps for later. Add the ghee. Stir-fry the seeds and turmeric for 10 seconds, add the garlic and stir-fry for 30 seconds. Add the curry powder and a tablespoon or two of milk and stir-fry for a couple of minutes.

2. Add the onion flakes, then add the remaining milk spoonful by spoonful over a minute to keep the sizzle going and avoid burning, stir-frying all the while.

3. Add the cooked lobster meat and half the cream and stir-fry for a couple of minutes, then add the shrimps, prawn ballichow, coriander, ground almonds, garam masala and the rest of the cream. When all the ingredients are mixed in the texture should be lusciously creamy and not too dry. If it is dry, add water little by little until you have achieved the right texture.

4. Simmer for a few minutes, then add salt to taste and serve.

Kerala Crab Curry

—— SERVES 2 ——

Kerala is at the southernmost tip of India. The sun always shines, and the people always smile. Maybe it's because the food is always good. It is lighter than the food of the north and often blended with that fruit of the palm – the coconut. For speed, the secret weapons in this recipe are a mixture of creamed coconut and coconut milk powder. Crabmeat just sings with such spicing. Serve with plain rice and chutneys. Try it and see.

◆

3 tablespoons sesame or soya oil
2–4 cloves garlic, chopped
4oz (110g) spring onions (leaves and bulbs), chopped
1–2 fresh green chillies, chopped
10–12 curry leaves, dried or fresh
1oz (25g) creamed coconut, chopped
4 tablespoons coconut milk powder
1 tablespoon prawn ballichow
1 tablespoon chopped red pepper
½ lb (225g) white crabmeat
4oz (110g) brown crabmeat

salt to taste
2 limes, quartered

SPICES
1 teaspoon mustard seeds
1 teaspoon sesame seeds
⅓ teaspoon lovage seeds
½ teaspoon chopped dried red chillies
⅓ teaspoon mango powder
⅓ teaspoon turmeric
½ teaspoon ground coriander
½ teaspoon chilli powder

◆

1. Heat the oil in a wok or karahi. Stir-fry the **spices** for 10 seconds. Add the garlic and stir-fry for 10 seconds more, then add the spring onions and chillies and stir-fry for a couple of minutes. Don't allow any sticking.

2. Add 7fl oz (200ml) water and the curry leaves and bring to a simmer, then stir-fry in the creamed coconut followed by the coconut milk powder.

3. Add the prawn ballichow, pepper and crabmeats. The mixture should be mobile, between runny and creamy. Add a little more water if it needs it.

4. Stir-fry for about 5 minutes, then add salt to taste. Serve with the lime quarters.

Goan Prawn Curry

—— SERVES 2 ——

Goans love the tart taste of vinegar and the piquancy of red chilli blended with warm spices and cashew nuts, and laced with wine. Follow this recipe, and you will have the magic of Goa at your fingertips in under 20 minutes. Serve with plain rice or bread.

12oz (350g) medium-size prawns, cooked and shelled
4 tablespoons soya or sunflower oil
½ teaspoon white cummin seeds
½ teaspoon coriander seeds
½ teaspoon chopped dried red chilli
2 teaspoons bottled minced garlic
1 teaspoon bottled minced ginger
4 tablespoons fried dried onion flakes
1 teaspoon tomato purée
2 tablespoons coconut milk powder
1 tablespoon chopped fresh green coriander leaves

1–2 fresh red chillies, sliced
12 cashew nuts, finely chopped or coarsely ground
4fl oz (100ml) port or Madeira
salt to taste

SPICE PASTE

1 tablespoon vinegar (any type)
1 teaspoon chilli powder
½ teaspoon paprika
½ teaspoon ground coriander
½ teaspoon mango powder
½ teaspoon dried fenugreek leaves

1. Combine the **spice paste** ingredients in a non-metallic bowl, adding a little water to make the mixture pourable.

2. Heat the oil in a wok or karahi. Stir-fry the seeds and chilli for 10 seconds. Add the spice paste (it will hiss and splutter) and stir-fry for a minute. Add the garlic and ginger and stir-fry for a minute.

3. Add the onion flakes. Where they have absorbed the liquid in the pan (which happens quickly), add just enough water to stop the sizzling.

4. Stir in the prawns and, as the sizzling starts again, stir-fry in the tomato purée, coconut milk powder, fresh coriander, chilli and cashew nuts. Cook for about 3 minutes.

5. The mixture should now be quite dry, but it must not stick to the pan. Add a little water if it does. Maintain a brisk stir-fry for a couple more minutes, then add the port or Madeira and salt to taste. Serve as soon as it is hot.

Bangladeshi Mach Ghol

—— SERVES 2 ——

Bangladeshi food is 'coming out' in Britain. For years it has been unknown, and despite the fact that nearly all the owners of UK Indian restaurants are from Bangladesh, they have concentrated on Punjabi and Moghul dishes which, good though they are, could not be more different from their own food. Fish, bones and all, is important to Bangladeshis. Here I re-create the divine subtle tastes of their food using panch phoran (Bengali five spice mixture, see page 8). However, I have omitted the bones.

2 tablespoons soya or sunflower oil
1 teaspoon white poppy seeds
1 teaspoon Bengali five spice mixture (see page 8)
1 teaspoon Dijon mustard
½ teaspoon turmeric
1 fresh green chilli, finely chopped
2–4 cloves garlic, chopped
3oz (75g) spring onions (leaves and bulbs), chopped

2 plaice fillets, each weighing about 7oz (200g)
1 tablespoon desiccated coconut
2 tablespoons coconut milk powder
1 tablespoon mango pickle, finely chopped
1 tablespoon chopped fresh green coriander leaves
salt to taste

1. Heat the oil in a wok or karahi. Stir-fry the seeds and the five spice mixture for 10 seconds. Add the mustard, turmeric and chilli and continue stir-frying for 30 seconds. Add the garlic and spring onions and continue to stir-fry for a couple more minutes.

2. Add 7fl oz (200ml) water and bring to a simmer.

3. Add the fish and let it simmer for 5 minutes, stirring gently from time to time.

4. Add all the remaining ingredients except the salt and bring to a simmer again.

5. Stir until the fish is cooked (a minimum of 5 another minutes). Add salt to taste and serve.

Malabar Coastal Fish Curry

—— SERVES 2 ——

The Malabar coast is in southwestern India where fishing is a major industry. Fish caught in the morning must be cooked by lunchtime or it would go off in the heat. With our fridge-freezers, we don't have that problem. Here flat fish is 'poached' in a frying pan, in coconut milk that has been coloured pale yellow by the addition of turmeric and made savoury with South Indian spices and lime pickle.

2 tablespoons sesame oil
½ teaspoon turmeric
3oz (75g) onion, finely sliced
1 tablespoon lime pickle, finely chopped
1 teaspoon yellow mustard powder
14fl oz (400ml) can coconut milk
10–12 curry leaves, fresh or dried
2 lemon sole fillets, each weighing about 7oz (200g)

salt to taste
4–6 lime wedges
freshly ground black pepper

SPICES
1 teaspoon mustard seeds
½ teaspoon coriander seeds
½ teaspoon white cummin seeds

1. Heat the oil in a large frying pan. Stir-fry the turmeric for 10 seconds. Add the **spices** and continue stir-frying for 30 seconds.

2. Add the onion and stir-fry for a further 3–4 minutes.

3. Add the lime pickle, mustard, coconut milk and curry leaves. Bring to a simmer, then add the fish and simmer for 10–15 minutes (or until cooked). Add salt to taste. Serve with the lime wedges and a twist of black pepper.

CHAPTER 8

♦

VEGETABLE AND LENTIL DISHES

Nothing does vegetables more proud than the spices of India. As most of us like our vegetable curries as side dishes, these ten recipes have been portioned as a accompaniments. They should be served with a main course dish from another chapter, together with rice and/or bread. If you want an all-vegetarian meal, however, either double the quantities or have two or three of these dishes with rice and/or bread.

Vegetable Bhuna Bhaji

—— SERVES 2 as an accompaniment ——

Any vegetable is known as a bhaji when it is curried. And bhuna is a style of cooking (dry-frying). To create this dish you can use any kind you want. My choice here is carrot, peas, green beans and sweetcorn (or frozen mixed vegetables) with celery.

◆

3 tablespoons soya or sunflower oil
2 teaspoons home-made curry powder (see page 7)
2 teaspoons bottled minced garlic
2oz (50g) spring onions (leaves and bulbs), chopped
1 tablespoon chopped red pepper
2 teaspoons brinjal (aubergine) pickle, chopped
1 teaspoon mango pickle, chopped

1 teaspoon tomato purée
½ teaspoon horseradish sauce
5oz (150g) mixed vegetables (peas, beans, carrot, sweetcorn)
2oz (50g) celery, chopped into small pieces
2 teaspoons chopped fresh green coriander leaves
½ teaspoon garam masala (see page 6)
salt to taste

◆

1. Heat the oil in a wok or karahi. Stir-fry the curry powder for 30 seconds. Add the garlic and continue stir-frying for 30 seconds. Add 2–3 tablespoons water and, when hot, add the spring onions and pepper. Stir-fry for 3 minutes.

2. Mix in the pickles, tomato purée and horseradish sauce, then add the vegetables, fresh coriander and garam masala and stir-fry until the mixture sizzles. Then add just enough water to create a dryish curry consistency and simmer for 3–4 minutes. Add salt to taste and serve.

Vegetable Jalfrezi Bhaji

—— SERVES 2 as an accompaniment ——

This version of a bhaji makes an interesting comparison with the previous recipe. The aubergine, tomato, courgettes and onion in the canned ratatouille make it ideal for a quick conversion to curry in a jalfrezi style stir-fry.

❖

2 tablespoons soya or sunflower oil
½ teaspoon white cummin seeds
½ teaspoon black mustard seeds
1 teaspoon garlic pickle, chopped
2 teaspoons home-made curry powder (see page 7)
4 tablespoons fried dried onion flakes
1 × 8oz (255g) can ratatouille

1 teaspoon ginger pickle, chopped
1 teaspoon brinjal (aubergine) pickle, chopped
2 teaspoons chopped fresh green coriander leaves
½ teaspoon garam masala (see page 6)
salt to taste

❖

1. Heat the oil in a wok or karahi. Stir-fry the seeds and garlic pickle for 30 seconds. Add the curry powder and stir-fry for 30 seconds more.

2. Add the onion flakes and, as soon as they are sizzling (a few seconds), add the ratatouille, ginger and brinjal pickles, fresh coriander and garam masala. Add salt to taste and serve as soon as it is hot.

Vegetable Indonesian Bhaji

—— **SERVES** 2 as an accompaniment ——

This third version of a bhaji also uses someone else's preparation to save time. Here it is fresh, mixed, prepared stir-fry vegetables – these are readily available at quality supermarkets and contain (usually) baby sweetcorn, bamboo shoots, bean sprouts, carrot, peppers and onion. Instead of turning them into a Chinese dish, I have created a rapid, stir-fried Indonesian curry.

2 tablespoons sesame oil
2–3 cloves garlic, sliced
1 inch (2.5cm) cube fresh ginger, sliced
½ (225g) ready prepared stir-fry
  vegetables
4fl oz (100ml) canned coconut milk
1 tablespoon peanut butter (optional)
½ teaspoon soy sauce
½ teaspoon hoisin sauce
½ teaspoon tomato purée

1 teaspoon brinjal (aubergine) pickle
salt to taste

SPICES
⅓ teaspoon fennel seeds
⅓ teaspoon sesame seeds
3–4 cloves, crushed
½ teaspoon home-made curry powder
  (see page 7)
¼ teaspoon ground cinnamon
¼ teaspoon turmeric

1. Heat the oil in a wok or karahi. Stir-fry the **spices** for 20 seconds. Add the garlic and ginger and stir-fry for a further minute or so.

2. Add the vegetables and mix them in rapidly. Stir-fry for about a minute to 'singe' them, then add the coconut milk, peanut butter if using, soy sauce, hoisin sauce, tomato purée and brinjal pickle. Add salt to taste.

3. Stir-fry for a few minutes until hot, then serve.

Mushroom Bhaji

—— SERVES 2 as an accompaniment ——

With an ever-increasing range of wild and cultivated mushrooms available in food stores, you can have as much fun with this recipe as you wish. For example, the other day I spotted a pack containing four or five different types of wild mushroom. The different varieties add zest to this recipe and their flavours, far from being drowned by the spices, are enhanced by them. The minimal cooking time of the mushrooms ensures they remain crisp and full of flavour rather than going soggy. If you only have button mushrooms they still make a splendid curry.

½lb (225g) mushrooms (any type or combination)
1 tablespoon vegetable ghee
1 tablespoon butter
½ teaspoon white cummin seeds
1 teaspoon bottled minced garlic
1 tablespoon chopped red or yellow pepper
1 fresh green chilli, shredded

3–4 spring onions (leaves and bulbs), finely chopped
1 tablespoon fresh mint leaves
1½ teaspoons home-made curry powder (see page 7)
2 teaspoons coconut milk powder
1 teaspoon garam masala (see page 6)
salt to taste

1. Wash and dry the mushrooms. Peel them only if they are dirty or dry. Chop or slice them.

2. Heat the ghee and butter in a wok or karahi. Stir-fry the cummin seeds for 10 seconds. Add the garlic, pepper and chilli and stir-fry for 1 minute.

3. Add the spring onions and mint leaves and continue stir-frying for a couple more minutes.

4. Add the curry powder and, when sizzling, about 4 tablespoons water.

5. Add the mushrooms and stir-fry them briskly, ensuring they all get evenly coated. (They are very absorbent so this needs speed and deftness). Then lower the heat and simmer for a minimum of 3 minutes.

6. Add the coconut milk powder, garam masala and salt to taste. Simmer for another minute and serve.

Cottage Cheese and Pea Curry

——— SERVES 2 as an accompaniment ———

Indian cheese is called paneer. It is time consuming to make, but is nutritionally good as well as being something quite different on the table. Here I have substituted cottage cheese for the paneer in the famous Indian dish, Mattar Paneer, and used frozen peas. This recipe, great as an accompaniment, takes almost no time at all to make.

◆

2 tablespoons butter
½ teaspoon white cummin seeds
⅓ teaspoon coriander seeds
⅓ teaspoon turmeric
2–3 cloves garlic, chopped
1 teaspoon home-made curry powder
   (see page 7)
2–3 spring onion bulbs, chopped

4oz (110g) frozen peas
2 teaspoons chopped fresh green
   coriander leaves
2 teaspoons chopped fresh mint
1 teaspoon garam masala (see page 6)
4oz (110g) cottage cheese
salt to taste

◆

1. Heat the butter in a wok or karahi. Stir-fry the seeds and turmeric for 20 seconds. Add the garlic and curry powder and stir-fry for 30 seconds more.

2. Add the spring onions and frozen peas and stir-fry for about 3 minutes (enough time to thaw the peas).

3. Add the fresh coriander, mint and garam masala and stir them in, then add the cottage cheese. Check for salt and add some if needed.

4. Stir until hot then serve.

Aloo Ghobi Sag

—— SERVES 2 as an accompaniment ——

The combination of potato (aloo), cauliflower (ghobi) and spinach (sag) makes a classic curry dish from northern India and Pakistan. These three super ingredients are intertwined with savoury Punjabi spices in this quick-to-make version.

3oz (75g) cauliflower florets
2 tablespoons vegetable or butter ghee
½ teaspoon fennel seeds
⅓ teaspoon coriander seeds
1 teaspoon garlic pickle
1 teaspoon home-made curry powder (see page 7)
3 tablespoons Greek yoghurt

1 teaspoon dried fenugreek leaves
6 oz (175g) spinach leaves, chopped
1 tablespoon butter
6–8 small potatoes, canned or boiled
1 tablespoon chopped fresh green coriander leaves
1 teaspoon garam masala (see page 6)
salt to taste

1. Soften the cauliflower florets in boiling water or in the microwave.

2. Heat the ghee in a wok or karahi. Stir-fry the seeds for 30 seconds. Add the garlic pickle and curry powder and stir-fry for a further minute.

3. Add the yoghurt, fenugreek leaves, spinach and butter and stir-fry for a couple of minutes until the spinach has softened and blended in.

4. Add the potatoes, cauliflower florets, fresh coriander, garam masala and just enough water to keep things mobile.

5. When everything is hot right through, salt to taste and serve.

Variation   Substitute broccoli for the cauliflower.

Fast Bombay Potatoes

—— SERVES 2 as an accompaniment ——

Nothing improves potatoes more than a tasty curry gravy. This combination is so popular that Indian restaurants have devised a name for it ... Bombay potatoes. The quickest way to make the dish is to re-heat already cooked potatoes. Alternatively, canned ones can be used.

3 tablespoons vegetable or butter ghee

2 teaspoons garlic pickle

1 teaspoon home-made curry powder (see page 7)

4 tablespoons fried dried onion flakes

4 tablespoons milk

1 teaspoon tomato purée

2 teaspoons chopped red pepper

½–1 teaspoon chopped green chilli

1 teaspoon garam masala (see page 6)

10–12 small new potatoes, boiled

2 tablespoons Greek yoghurt

1–2 teaspoons chopped fresh green coriander leaves

salt to taste

1. Heat the ghee in a wok or karahi. Stir-fry the garlic pickle and curry powder for a minute or so. Add the onion flakes and mix them in, then add the milk. Stir-fry for about 1 minute.

2. Mix in the tomato purée, pepper, chilli and garam masala, then add the potatoes and stir-fry for 2–3 minutes.

3. Add the yoghurt and fresh coriander and stir-fry for a further couple of minutes. Add salt to taste and serve.

Madrasi Sambar (Lentil Curry)

—— **SERVES** 2 as an accompaniment ——

In the south of India they combine their passion for vegetables, lentils and chillies in the classic dish, sambar. In this quick version, based on a recipe from Madras, I have achieved its typical tart flavours by using lime pickle. Serve with plain rice and chutneys and a main course curry.

◆

7 floz (200ml) vegetable stock or water
2oz (50g) split and polished red lentils
2 teaspoons desiccated coconut
1 fresh red chilli
10–12 curry leaves, fresh or dried
2 tablespoons soya or sunflower oil
½ teaspoon mustard seeds
½ teaspoon white cummin seeds
¼ teaspoon black cummin seeds
¼ teaspoon sesame seeds

1 teaspoon garlic pickle, chopped
1 teaspoon lime pickle, chopped
1 teaspoon home-made curry powder
  (see page 7)
2oz (50g) mixed vegetables and their
  liquid from a can
2 teaspoons chopped fresh green
  coriander leaves
salt to taste

◆

1. Bring the stock or water to the boil, then add the lentils, coconut, chilli and curry leaves and simmer for about 20 minutes. Spoon off any scum which may form.

2. Heat the oil in a wok or karahi. Stir-fry the seeds for 20 seconds. Add the garlic and lime pickles and curry powder and stir-fry for a further minute. Strain the vegetables and add them to the wok. When sizzling, add the coriander and the vegetable liquid.

3. Add the contents of the other pan to the wok. Simmer for a couple of minutes more. Add salt to taste and serve.

Chole (Chick Pea Curry)

—— SERVES 2 as an accompaniment ——

For 'after-workers' who have to quick-cook curries, canned chick peas are one of life's sweet blessings. This curry, based on a Kashmiri recipe – chole, pronounced 'choalay' – is enhanced with aromatic spices, ginger, tomato and peppers. Note the use of humous as a thickener. Serve with bread or rice and chutneys and a main course curry.

♦

10oz (300g) canned chick peas, weighed after straining (reserve the liquid; see Steps 1 and 2)
2 tablespoons butter ghee
2 teaspoons garlic pickle, chopped
1 tablespoon ginger pickle, chopped
2 teaspoons tomato purée
2 tablespoons butter
6 tablespoons dried onion flakes
1 teaspoon vinegared mint
6–8 cherry tomatoes, halved
1 tablespoon chopped green pepper
1–2 red chillies

1 tablespoon Greek yoghurt
2 tablespoons humous (or more)
1 tablespoon chopped fresh green coriander leaves
1 teaspoon garam masala (see page 6)
salt to taste

SPICES
½ teaspoon white cummin seeds
⅓ teaspoon coriander seeds
2 brown cardamoms, halved
4 cloves, crushed
2 bay leaves

♦

1. Heat the ghee in a wok or karahi. Stir-fry the **spices** for 30 seconds, then add the pickles and stir-fry for about a minute. Add a spoonful or two of the chick pea liquid, then mix in the tomato purée. Add the butter and onion flakes and stir-fry for a couple of minutes.

2. Add another spoonful or two of the chick pea liquid, this time adding the mint, tomatoes, pepper and chilli. When the mixture is sizzling, add the chick peas, yoghurt and remaining chick pea liquid.

3. Depending on the heat and the amount of liquid from the can, the mixture should now drop easily off a spoon. (If not add a little water.)

4. Add the humous to thicken the curry a little. Exactly how much is needed will depend on the above, so be flexible. Then add the fresh coriander, garam masala and salt to taste.

5. Stir and simmer for a short while more to ensure that everything is hot, then serve.

Quick Tasty Dhal

—— SERVES 2 as an accompaniment ——

Dhal or lentil dishes are immensely popular in India, so much so that whereas we think in terms of curry and rice, the norm there is curry, rice and dhal. This tasty dhal is so nice that you can omit the curry, as Indians often do, and enjoy it just with plain rice and chutneys. It makes a totally nutritious, delicious, filling, cheap and satisfying meal. I use red split lentils here, because they are the quickest to cook. Even so, this recipe has one of the longest cooking times in the book: 40 minutes. Most of this is unattended simmering on the stove. However, this dish freezes well, so one tip is to cook several batches, simply by doubling, quadrupling, etc. the quantities, and freezing them in suitable containers.

5fl oz (150ml) canned consommé or water

2½oz (70g) split and polished red lentils

3 tablespoons butter ghee

2 teaspoons garlic pickle

1 teaspoon ginger pickle

3 tablespoons fried dried onion flakes

1 tablespoon Greek yoghurt

2 tablespoons humous

1 teaspoon dried fenugreek leaves

1 teaspoon garam masala (see page 6)

2 teaspoons tomato ketchup

salt to taste

---

1. Bring the consommé or water to the boil, add the lentils and simmer for 20 minutes on low heat.

2. Add all the remaining ingredients, including the salt, and simmer until the dhal is the texture you like. This will take about another 20 minutes (the longer the cooking, the more puréed the lentils become). Watch the water content. If at any time the lentils get dry enough to stick, add enough water to 'release' them.

CHAPTER 9

◆

QUICK, POPULAR SAUCES

I've been considering pasta. It is now Britain's most popular cook-at-home food, ahead even of curry. The reason for its success, I believe, is its simplicity. In one pan you boil the pasta, in another you make a sauce. They are both ready to eat minutes later and you simply combine one with the other for a marvellous meal.

Suppose we could do the same with curry. In one pan you cook the rice, in the other you create a tasty sauce. Forget about meat, chicken, fish, prawns, or vegetables. Just cook the sauce (in the time it takes to cook the rice), pour it over the rice (or indeed pasta), mix it in well, and eat it. Here then, are pour-and-mix sauce versions of twelve of the most popular restaurant curries.

Ceylonese Sauce

—— SERVES 2 as a pour-and-mix sauce ——

This restaurant-style interpretation of the tart, hot and coconut-creamy curries of Sri Lanka uses coconut milk, lime (fresh and pickled) and chilli. Serve with plain or flavoured rice.

150g (5oz) basmati rice	5 floz (150ml) canned coconut milk
2 tablespoons soya or sunflower oil	½oz (15g) creamed coconut, chopped
1 teaspoon black mustard seeds	10–12 curry leaves, fresh or dried
1 tablespoon home-made curry powder (see page 7)	1 teaspoon lime pickle, finely chopped
⅛ teaspoon asafoetida (optional)	1 teaspoon chilli pickle, finely chopped
1 tablespoon garlic pickle, finely chopped	salt to taste
6 tablespoons dried onion flakes, crumbled	2–3 fresh limes
	chilli powder
	freshly ground black pepper

1. Cook the rice according to one of the recipes in Chapter 10.

2. Meanwhile, heat the oil in a wok or karahi. Stir-fry the mustard seeds for 10 seconds. Add the curry powder, asafoetida if using and garlic pickle and stir-fry for another minute. Add 2 tablespoons water and the onion flakes. Mix in briskly and add 2 tablespoons water to prevent burning.

3. Add the coconut milk and creamed coconut, curry leaves and lime and chilli pickles and simmer for a few minutes – just enough time to allow the sauce to thicken but not stick. Add salt to taste.

4. To serve, mix the sauce into the rice. Squeeze on the juice from the limes and sprinkle with the chilli powder and a few twists of pepper.

Dhansak Sauce

—— SERVES 2 as a pour-and-mix sauce ——

The restaurant interpretation of this favourite Bombay Parsee curry is lentil-based and savoury, hot and slightly sweet. This quick-to-make version uses chick peas and humous instead of lentils, ratatouille for the savoury taste and sugar and chilli. Serve with plain or flavoured rice.

150g (5oz) basmati rice
3 tablespoons butter ghee
1 teaspoon garlic pickle, finely
    chopped
2 teaspoons ginger pickle, finely
    chopped
1 teaspoon dark muscovado sugar
4 tablespoons tomato juice
2 tablespoons dried onion flakes
3oz (75g) canned ratatouille
3oz (75g) canned chick peas, mashed
    with their liquid
2–3 tablespoons humous
2 tablespoons puréed spinach

1 teaspoon garam masala (see page 6)
salt to taste
2 lemons

GARNISH
chopped fresh green coriander leaves

SPICES
½ teaspoon chilli powder
1 teaspoon ground coriander
½ teaspoon ground cummin
⅓ teaspoon ground cinnamon
⅓ teaspoon fennel seeds
¼ teaspoon green cardamom seeds

---

1. Cook the rice according to one of the recipes in Chapter 10.

2. Meanwhile, heat the ghee in a wok or karahi. Stir-fry the **spices** for 30 seconds. Add the garlic and ginger pickles and sugar and continue to stir-fry for another minute. Add half the tomato juice and the onion. Mix in briskly and add the remaining tomato juice to prevent burning.

3. Add the ratatouille, chick peas and humous and mix in well (adding a little water if needed to keep things mobile). Stir and simmer for 3–4 minutes.

4. Add the spinach, garam masala and salt to taste and simmer for at least a couple more minutes. You should now have a sauce which drops easily off the spoon. Add water if necessary to achieve this.

5. To serve, mix into the rice and squeeze on the juice from the lemons. Sprinkle with the coriander leaves.

Kashmiri Sauce

—— SERVES 2 as a pour-and-mix sauce ——

Long ago, the owners of curry restaurants decided that Kashmiri curries contained fruit – and chose lychees, which come from China, not Kashmir. What authentic Kashmiri food uses prolifically is lotus, not lychees! Nevertheless, bowing to the restaurants, here is a Kashmiri interpretation of a pour-and-mix sauce, complete with canned lychees enhanced with aromatic spices. Serve with plain or flavoured rice.

◆

150g (5oz) basmati rice
3 tablespoons butter ghee
1 teaspoon white poppy seeds
2 teaspoons garlic pickle, finely chopped
1 teaspoon ginger pickle, finely chopped
1 teaspoon white sugar
4fl oz (100ml) tomato juice
4 tablespoons dried onion flakes
1 teaspoon red pesto sauce

6fl oz (150ml) milk
1 tablespoon ground almonds
4 canned lychees, chopped
1 tablespoon chopped fresh green coriander leaves
salt to taste

GARNISH
garam masala
chopped fresh mint leaves

◆

1. Cook the rice according to one of the recipes in Chapter 10.

2. Meanwhile, heat the ghee in a wok or karahi. Stir-fry the poppy seeds for 20 seconds. Add the garlic and ginger pickles and sugar and continue to stir-fry for another minute. Add half the tomato juice and the onion flakes. Mix in briskly and add the remaining tomato juice to prevent burning. Add the pesto and milk.

3. Add the ground almonds, lychees and fresh coriander and stir-fry until heated through. Add salt to taste.

4. To serve, mix into the rice and sprinkle with the garam masala and mint leaves.

Korma Sauce

—— SERVES 2 as a pour-and-mix sauce ——

The true korma is aromatic and very mild as the meat is marinated in yoghurt before being slow-cooked to a creamy result. The restaurant korma, and this version, use evaporated milk, cream and coconut to achieve a rich mild curry. Serve with plain or flavoured rice.

150g (5oz) basmati rice
3 tablespoons butter ghee
1½ teaspoons garlic pickle, finely chopped
½ teaspoon ginger pickle, finely chopped
6 tablespoons dried onion flakes
2fl oz (50ml) single cream
3 tablespoons evaporated milk
½ teaspoon saffron powder
1 tablespoon coconut milk powder
2 teaspoons ground almonds
1 teaspoon garam masala (see page 6)

1 tablespoon chopped fresh green coriander leaves
salt to taste

GARNISH
1 tablespoon flaked almonds, toasted

SPICES
½ teaspoon white cummin seeds
¼ teaspoon black cummin seeds
½ teaspoon fennel seeds
¼ teaspoon green cardamom seeds
½ inch (5cm) piece cassia bark
2 bay leaves

1. Cook the rice according to one of the recipes in Chapter 10.

2. Meanwhile, heat the ghee in a wok or karahi. Stir-fry the **spices** for 30 seconds. Add the garlic and ginger pickles and stir-fry for 30 seconds more. Add 4 tablespoons water and the onion flakes. These will be quickly absorbed and you will need to add more water quickly to prevent burning, stirring all the time.

3. Mix in the cream and evaporated milk and stir-fry for a few minutes more. You will probably need to add a little extra water.

4. Add the saffron and coconut milk powders, ground almonds, garam masala and fresh coriander and simmer for 3–4 minutes stirring (and adding splashes of water) as needed. Add salt to taste.

5. To serve, mix into the rice and garnish with the toasted flaked almonds.

Malaysian Sauce

—— SERVES 2 as a pour-and-mix sauce ——

True Malaysian curries link Indian techniques with Chinese ingredients. The restaurant interpretation is to produce a smooth, hot, tangy curry with a sweet undertone. This is achieved by using coconut milk, chilli, ginger and pineapple. Serve with plain or flavoured rice.

◆

150g (5oz) basmati rice
2 tablespoons soya oil
2–3 cloves garlic, sliced
2 inch (5cm) piece fresh ginger, sliced
1 tablespoon home-made curry powder (see page 7)
6 tablespoons tomato juice
6 tablespoons fried dried onion flakes, crumbled
1 tablespoon brinjal (aubergine) pickle, chopped
1 tablespoon peanut butter
3fl oz (75ml) canned coconut milk
1 tablespoon creamed coconut, chopped

1–2 fresh red chillies, chopped
12–20 fresh green coriander leaves
4–6 canned pineapple chunks
salt to taste

SPICES
1 teaspoon Bengali five spice mixture (see page 8)
½ teaspoon turmeric

GARNISH
fresh green coriander leaves
lemon wedges for squeezing

◆

1. Cook the rice according to one of the recipes in Chapter 10.

2. Meanwhile, heat the oil in a wok or karahi. Stir-fry the **spices** for 30 seconds. Add the garlic and ginger and stir-fry for a further minute. Add the curry powder and 2 tablespoons of the tomato juice, and stir-fry for a further 30 seconds. Add the onion flakes, brinjal pickle and the rest of the tomato juice and stir well for a minute more.

3. Add all the remaining ingredients except the salt and stir-fry for 3–4 minutes to allow the sauce to thicken but not stick.

4. Add salt to taste and simmer for at least a couple more minutes. You should now have a nice mobile sauce which drops easily off the spoon. Add water if necessary to achieve this.

5. Mix into the rice and garnish with a sprinkling of coriander leaves and a squeeze of lemon juice.

Madras Sauce

—— SERVES 2 as a pour-and-mix sauce ——

Although you won't find a Madras curry anywhere in Madras, in Indian restaurants it has become synonymous with hot tasty curries. Chilli, of course, achieves the heat with tomatoes and ground almonds giving quality to the taste and texture, all captured in this pour-and-mix sauce. Serve with plain or flavoured rice.

150g (5oz) basmati rice
3 tablespoons vegetable oil
1 tablespoon home-made curry
 powder (see page 7)
1 teaspoon chilli powder
2 teaspoons garlic pickle, chopped
1 teaspoon ginger pickle, chopped
6 tablespoons fried dried onion flakes
1 teaspoon dried fenugreek leaves
1 tablespoon tomato purée
1 tablespoon tomato ketchup
4 canned tomatoes, chopped

1 tablespoon coconut milk powder
1 tablespoon ground almonds
1 teaspoon white sugar
1 tablespoon chopped fresh green
 coriander leaves
salt to taste

GARNISH
lemon wedges for squeezing
chilli powder
twists of lemon peel

---

1. Cook the rice according to one of the recipes in Chapter 10.

2. Meanwhile, heat the oil in a wok or karahi. Stir-fry the curry and chilli powders for 1 minute, adding 2 tablespoons water as you go. Add the garlic and ginger pickles (and a little more water to prevent sticking) and stir-fry for another minute.

3. Add the onion flakes, fenugreek leaves, tomato purée and ketchup and stir-fry briskly for another minute. Add the tomatoes, coconut milk powder, ground almonds and sugar and just enough water to keep the mixture cohesive. Stir-fry for 3 minutes or so.

4. Add the fresh coriander and salt to taste.

5. To serve, mix into the rice. Squeeze on the juice from the lemon wedges and garnish with a sprinkling of chilli powder and twists of lemon peel.

Muglai Sauce

—— SERVES 2 as a pour-and-mix sauce ——

The world's most opulent rulers, the Moghuls or Mugals (who ruled in India during the Tudor period in England) enjoyed equally opulent food. The restaurant interpretation of this curry uses cream, saffron and almonds. Serve with plain or flavoured rice.

♦

150g (5oz) basmati rice
4 tablespoons milk
10–15 saffron strands
3 tablespoons butter ghee
2 tablespoons pine kernels
1 tablespoon garlic pickle, chopped
1 tablespoon home-made curry
  powder (see page 7)
3fl oz (75ml) single cream
6 tablespoons fried dried flaked onions
1 tablespoon ground almonds
4 fresh mint leaves, chopped
10–12 fresh green coriander leaves

1 teaspoon garam masala (page 6)
1 teaspoon mango chutney, chopped

SPICES
½ teaspoon white cummin seeds
¼ teaspoon black cummin seeds
1–2 star anise
4–6 green cardamom seeds
4–6 cloves
1 inch (2.5cm) piece cassia bark

GARNISH
20–30 flaked almonds, toasted
single cream

♦

1. Cook the rice according to one of the recipes in Chapter 10.

2. Meanwhile, warm the milk with the saffron strands over low heat for 30 seconds, or in the microwave for about 10 seconds. To infuse the colour, mash the strands around with the back of a spoon.

3. Heat the ghee in a wok or karahi. Stir-fry the pine kernels for 30 seconds. Add the **spices** and stir-fry for 30 seconds. Add the garlic pickle and curry powder and 2 tablespoons of the cream and stir-fry for another minute. Add the onion flakes and, when sizzling, the saffron and milk. Stir-fry until the mixture dries out (but doesn't burn).

4. Add the rest of the cream, the ground almonds, mint and coriander leaves, garam masala and mango chutney and stir-fry until hot. A little water will probably be needed to keep things cohesive. Add salt to taste.

5. Mix into the rice and garnish with almonds and a curl of cream.

Patia Sauce

—— SERVES 2 as a pour-and-mix sauce ——

Originally created centuries ago by the Parsees, patia combines heat and sweetness in a rich, dark red sauce. In restaurants this is achieved with chilli, sugar, paprika and tomato purée to which, in this pour-and-mix sauce version, I have added a few other taste enhancers. Serve with plain or flavoured rice.

◆

150g (5oz) basmati rice
2 tablespoons butter ghee
1 teaspoon bottled minced garlic, chopped
2 teaspoons ginger pickle, chopped
1 teaspoon dark muscovado sugar
2 tablespoons butter
6 tablespoons fried dried onion flakes
5fl oz (150ml) canned cream of tomato soup
1 teaspoon tomato purée
2 teaspoons tomato ketchup
2 teaspoons mango chutney, chopped
1 teaspoon Dijon mustard
1 teaspoon horseradish sauce
1 teaspoon red pesto
½ teaspoon mint jelly

1 tablespoon chopped fresh green coriander leaves
1 teaspoon garam masala (see page 6)
salt to taste

SPICES
1 teaspoon ground coriander
½ teaspoon ground cinnamon
¼ teaspoon ground cloves
1 teaspoon tandoori curry powder (see page 8)
1 teaspoon paprika
½–1 teaspoon chilli powder

GARNISH
matchstick crisps (optional)
desiccated coconut

◆

1. Cook the rice according to one of the recipes in Chapter 10.

2. Meanwhile, heat the ghee in a wok or karahi. Stir-fry the spices for 1 minute, adding 1–2 tablespoons water to keep them from sticking. Add the garlic, ginger pickle, sugar, butter and onion flakes and stir-fry for a couple more minutes. Add the tomato soup bit by bit while you do this.

3. Add all the remaining ingredients including salt to taste. Stir-fry for 2–3 minutes. Add a little water, if needed, to keep it mobile.

4. To serve, mix into the rice. Garnish with the matchstick crisps if wished and desiccated coconut.

Phal Sauce

—— SERVES 2 as a pour-and-mix sauce ——

Nowhere outside an Indian restaurant will you find the hottest curry: phal. It certainly doesn't exist in the real world of the sub-continent. Its potent red heat is achieved by using extra-hot chilli powder. Serve with plain or flavoured rice.

150g (5oz) basmati rice
3 tablespoons vegetable oil
1 teaspoon white cummin seeds
1 teaspoon paprika
2–3 teaspoons extra-hot chilli powder
1 teaspoon home-made curry powder
  (see page 7)
2 teaspoons garlic pickle, chopped
1 tablespoon chilli pickle, chopped
6 tablespoons dried onion flakes,
  crumbled

6 tablespoons tomato juice
1 tablespoon tomato ketchup
1–2 teaspoons bottled minced red chilli
1 teaspoon prepared English mustard
½ teaspoon dried mint
1 tablespoon chopped fresh green
  coriander leaves
salt to taste

GARNISH
1–2 fresh green chillies, shredded

1. Cook the rice according to one of the recipes in Chapter 10.

2. Meanwhile, heat the oil in a wok or karahi. Stir-fry the cummin seeds, paprika and chilli and curry powders. Add 2 tablespoons water and the pickles. Stir-fry for another minute.

3. Add the onion flakes and stir-fry them briskly in, then add the tomato juice. Stir-fry for a couple of minutes adding water little by little if necessary. Add all the remaining ingredients except the salt, bring to a simmer and add salt to taste.

4. To serve, mix into the rice and garnish with the green chillies.

Roghan Josh Sauce

—— SERVES 2 as a pour-and-mix sauce ——

There are two possible meanings for roghan. In Iranian it means ghee. In Kashmiri it means red. It is an aromatic Moghul dish and as the Moghuls spoke Persian and lived in Kashmir both meanings could apply. Restaurants play safe and cook roghan in ghee and add red ingredients (peppers, paprika and tomatoes). Josh, incidentally, means sauce. I have added a few extra touches to make this tasty version. Serve with plain or flavoured rice.

◆

150g (5oz) basmati rice
3 tablespoons butter ghee
2–3 cloves garlic, chopped
1 inch (2.5cm) cube ginger, shredded
about 10 tablespoons milk
4 tablespoons dried onion flakes
1 tablespoon bottled beetroot, mashed
5fl oz (150ml) canned cream of
 mushroom soup
1 tablespoon thinly sliced red pepper
1 tablespoon thinly sliced fresh green
 chilli
4 cherry tomatoes, quartered
1 tablespoon Greek yoghurt

1 tablespoon chopped fresh green
 coriander leaves
salt to taste

SPICES
½ teaspoon white cummin seeds
⅓ teaspoon black cummin seeds
2 black cardamom pods, halved
2 bay leaves
3 cloves, crushed
½ teaspoon fennel seeds
½ teaspoon paprika
½ teaspoon ground coriander

GARNISH
fresh green coriander leaves

◆

1. Cook the rice according to one of the recipes in Chapter 10.

2. Meanwhile, heat the ghee in a wok or karahi. Stir-fry the **spices** for 30 seconds. Add the garlic and stir-fry for 30 seconds more. Add the ginger and continue stir-frying for another 30 seconds.

3. Add 3 tablespoons of the milk and the onion flakes and beetroot. Add the remaining milk over a couple of minutes, stirring all the while.

4. Add all the remaining ingredients including salt to taste. Stir and simmer for about another 3 minutes.

5. To serve, mix into the rice and garnish with the coriander leaves.

Thai Green Curry Sauce

—— SERVES 2 as a pour-and-mix sauce ——

Of course you will not find Thai curries at Indian restaurants. But you will find them at Thai restaurants where they are really quite authentic. The runny sauce gets its colour from green ingredients (chilli, pepper, coriander and basil) although it is not a vibrant green. The fragrance of Thai food comes largely from lemon grass and basil leaves. Serve with plain or flavoured rice.

◆

150g (5oz) basmati rice
2 tablespoons soya oil
2 teaspoons bottled minced garlic
1 teaspoon bottled minced ginger
4oz (110g) spring onions (leaves and bulbs), sliced
2 pieces bottled or fresh lemon grass stalk
1 tablespoon sliced green pepper
1 teaspoon green pesto
1–2 fresh green chillies, chopped
1 tablespoon bottled minced coriander

1 tablespoon cooked prawns, mashed (optional)
3fl oz (75ml) canned coconut milk
10–12 fresh basil leaves, chopped
1 teaspoon light soy sauce
salt to taste
2–3 limes

GARNISH
1 large fresh red chilli, shredded, or miniature chillies

◆

1. Cook the rice according to one of the recipes in Chapter 10.

2. Meanwhile, heat the oil in a wok or karahi. Stir-fry the garlic and ginger for 30 seconds. Add the spring onions and lemon grass and continue to stir-fry for another minute. Add the pepper, pesto, chilli, coriander and prawns if using and stir-fry for a further minute.

3. Add the coconut milk and simmer for 2–3 minutes, stirring frequently, during which time the sauce will thicken a little. It must be runny rather than thick, so add a little water to keep things mobile.

4. Add the fresh basil leaves, soy sauce and salt to taste. Simmer and stir until the leaves soften (about another 2 minutes).

5. To serve, remove and discard the lemon grass and mix the sauce into the rice. Squeeze over the juice from the limes and garnish with the red chillies.

Vindaloo Sauce

—— SERVES 2 as a pour-and-mix sauce ——

This dish originated in Portuguese Goa where it combined vinegar and garlic with chillies. The restaurant interpretation latched on to the word aloo, meaning potato, but dropped the vinegar. The resultant very hot curry relies on chilli to achieve its strength, as does this pour-and-mix sauce. Serve with plain or flavoured rice.

150g (5oz) basmati rice
3 tablespoons vegetable oil
2 teaspoons home-made curry powder (see page 7)
1–2 teaspoons extra-hot chilli powder
2 teaspoons garlic pickle, chopped
1 teaspoon chilli pickle, chopped
6 tablespoons fried dried onion flakes
2 canned tomatoes, chopped
3fl oz (75ml) canned cream of tomato soup

½–1 teaspoon bottled minced red chilli
1 tablespoon chopped fresh green coriander leaves
2–3 small cooked potatoes, halved (optional)
salt to taste

GARNISH
fresh green coriander leaves
chopped fresh green chillies

1. Cook the rice according to one of the recipes in Chapter 10.

2. Meanwhile, heat the oil in a wok or karahi. Stir-fry the curry and chilli powders for 1 minute, adding 2 tablespoons water as you go. Add the pickles (and a little more water to prevent sticking) and stir-fry for another minute.

3. Add the onion flakes and tomatoes and mix well. Now stir in the tomato soup, spoonful by spoonful, keeping things sizzling, over the next 2 minutes.

4. Add the minced chilli, chopped fresh coriander and potatoes if using. Simmer for a couple more minutes, adding water if the sauce becomes too dry. Add salt to taste.

5. To serve, mix into the rice and garnish with the coriander leaves and chopped chillies.

CHAPTER 10

◆

RICE

Curry and rice are as immutable as sun and sky or health and happiness. We can scarcely imagine one without the other. Yet there are parts of India where the climate is wrong for rice growing and only bread is eaten with curries.

As bread takes time to make, I have avoided giving recipes for it in this book. Pre-cooked Indian breads can be bought, ready to heat, from an increasing number of supermarkets. Readily available pittas can be substituted for naan and are easily warmed in a toaster. Alternatively, you can resort to a takeaway.

Rice does not take a lot of time to cook – you can do it in less than 10 minutes, including rinsing. But to get fluffy grains, you will have to allow time for it to dry out after cooking (at least 30 minutes). However, I sometimes eat my rice straight after straining it and, although it is a little 'wet', it is quite acceptable. If you cook rice the day before and keep it in the fridge you can re-heat it quickly, simply by stir-frying. It can also be frozen successfully – just stir-fry the thawed rice and it will be almost as good as new.

Plain Boiled Rice

—— SERVES 2 (makes 2 portions) ——

Use basmati rice, follow this recipe accurately and you will have fragrant fluffy dry rice.

———————————————◆———————————————

5oz (150g) basmati rice
1½ pints (900ml) water

———————————————◆———————————————

1. Pick through the rice to remove grit and impurities.

2. Boil the water in a 3 pint (1.75 litre) pan. It is not necessary to salt it.

3. While the water is heating up, rinse the rice briskly with fresh cold water until most of the starch is washed out and the water runs clear.

4. Boil a kettle of water and run it through the rice at the final rinse. This minimizes the temperature reduction when you put the rice into the boiling water in the pan.

5. When the water is boiling properly, put the rice into the pan. Start timing. Put the lid on the pan until the water comes back to the boil, then remove the lid and stir frequently.

6. After about 6 minutes, taste a few grains. As soon as the centre is no longer brittle, but still has a good *al dente* bite to it, strain off the water. The rice should seem slightly undercooked. It takes 8–10 minutes from the moment you put the rice in the pan.

7. Shake off all the excess water, then place the strainer on a dry tea towel which will help remove the last of the water.

8. After a minute or so place the rice in a warmed serving dish. You can serve it now or, preferably, put it into a very low oven or warming drawer for at least 30 minutes and at most 90 minutes. As the rice dries the grains will separate and become fluffy.

9. Just before serving, fluff up the rice with a fork to aerate it and release the steam.

Fried Pullao Rice

—— SERVES 2 (makes 2 average-sized portions) ——

A simple method of making tasty pullao rice by stir-frying plain boiled rice.

---

2 teaspoons butter or vegetable ghee
5oz (150g) basmati rice, cooked and
   dried as in Plain Boiled Rice (see
   page 99)
½ teaspoon saffron powder

SPICES
½ teaspoon fennel seeds
¼ teaspoon green cardamom seeds

¼ teaspoon black cummin seeds
1 star anise
1 inch (2.5cm) piece cassia bark
1 bay leaf
1–2 cloves

GARNISH (optional)
1 teaspoon desiccated coconut

---

1. Heat the ghee in a wok or karahi and stir-fry the **spices** for about 30 seconds.

2. Lower the heat, add the cooked rice and saffron powder and stir-fry briskly until hot enough to eat. If the heat is too high the rice will stick and burn. Garnish with the coconut if wished and serve at once.

Pea Pullao Rice

—— SERVES 2 (makes 2 average-sized portions) ——

This involves nothing more nor less than the crafty addition of peas to Fried Pullao Rice.

Fried Pullao Rice (see above)
3 tablespoons cooked peas

Follow the recipe for Fried Pullao Rice recipe in its entirety. Add the peas when you put the rice into the wok (Step 2).

Mushroom Pullao Rice

—— SERVES 2 (makes 2 average-sized portions) ——

A further variation on Fried Pullao Rice. This time fresh raw mushrooms are added.

———————————————— ◆ ————————————————

Fried Pullao Rice (see page 100)
4–6 mushrooms (any type), cleaned, peeled as necessary and chopped

———————————————— ◆ ————————————————

Follow the recipe for Fried Pullao Rice in its entirety. Add the mushrooms when you put the rice into the wok (Step 2).

Garlic Pullao Rice

—— SERVES 2 (makes 2 average-sized portions) ——

Not for the fainthearted, nor to be taken if you wish to impress the boss the next day – but a simply delicious variation on Fried Pullao Rice. I have used garlic pickle.

———————————————— ◆ ————————————————

Fried Pullao Rice (see page 100)
1 tablespoon garlic pickle

———————————————— ◆ ————————————————

Follow the recipe for Fried Pullao Rice in its entirety. Add the garlic pickle when you put the rice into the wok (Step 2).

Pickle Rice

—— SERVES 2 (makes 2 average-sized portions) ——

The notion of adding pickle to rice is a good one (see Garlic Pullao Rice, page 101). At a pinch it's a meal in itself, certainly if you accompany it with a curry sauce from Chapter 9 and some chutneys.

◆

Fried Pullao Rice (see page 100)
1–2 tablespoons Indian pickle (lime, mango, mixed or brinjal), chopped

◆

Follow the recipe for Fried Pullao Rice in its entirety. Add the pickle when you put the rice into the wok (Step 2).

Cachumber Rice

—— SERVES 2 (makes 2 average-sized portions) ——

For this variant of Fried Pullao Rice I have simply added the full batch of Cachumber Salad Chutney from page 107.

◆

Fried Pullao Rice (see page 100)
Cachumber Salad Chutney (see page 107)

◆

Follow the Fried Pullao Rice recipe, adding the Cachumber Salad Chutney when you put the rice into the wok (Step 2).

Kitchri (Rice and Chick Peas)

—— **SERVES 2** (makes 2 average-sized portions) ——

Here I have mixed canned chick peas into Fried Pullao Rice to create Kitchri, the forerunner of kedgeree.

Fried Pullao Rice (see page 100)
2oz (50g) strained canned chick peas

Follow the recipe for Fried Pullao Rice in its entirety. Add the chick peas when you put the rice into the wok (Step 2).

Chicken Tikka Pullao

—— SERVES 2 ——

This variation of Fried Pullao Rice could become your favourite. You will need some cooked Instant Chicken Tikka from the recipe on page 27. We often have leftovers in the fridge and this is the ideal way to use them up. It is a meal in itself but a little dry, so accompany it with Quick Tasty Dhal (see page 84) and chutneys.

1 tablespoon butter ghee
½ teaspoon cummin seeds
2 teaspoons tandoori curry powder (see page 8)
2 spring onions (leaves and bulbs), chopped
½ tablespoon chopped red pepper
1 fresh green chilli, chopped (optional)
2 tablespoons yoghurt
1 teaspoon tomato purée
about 10oz (175g) Instant Chicken Tikka (see page 27), cut small

about 10oz (300g) Fried Pullao Rice (see page 100)
1 tablespoon chopped fresh green coriander leaves
1 teaspoon garam masala (see page 6)
salt to taste

GARNISH
snipped chives
flaked almonds

1. Heat the ghee in a wok or karahi. Fry the cummin seeds and curry powder for 10 seconds.

2. Add the spring onions, pepper and chilli, if using, and stir-fry for 3 minutes. Add the yoghurt and tomato purée and stir-fry for another minute.

3. Add the chicken tikka pieces and stir-fry for another 3 minutes.

4. Add the pullao rice and stir-fry carefully until it (and the chicken) is hot right through.

5. Add the fresh coriander and garam masala and stir-fry for a couple more minutes, then add salt to taste. Garnish with the chives and almonds and serve.

CHAPTER 11

◆

CHUTNEYS

Serious curryholics collect bottled Indian pickles. The usual ones are lime, brinjal (aubergine) and mango pickles. There is also a mixed version of these, and a chilli pickle for those who like it hot. On the mild side, there is mango chutney, that sweet and syrupy concoction which most people seem to enjoy. The collectors will tell you that many of these pickles vary quite markedly from manufacturer to manufacturer. It is a good idea to have at least some of these ready-made items in your cupboard. Indeed, I use them for cooking as well as for enjoying in their own right.

But India has much more up her sleeve to accompany curries: freshly made chutneys. That's what the following recipes are all about. They are quick to make, and go so very well with the recipes in this book that you could have more than one with each meal.

Dana Podine Purée

—— SERVES 2 ——

A tasty herby chutney, here made quickly with bottled products.

———————————— ◆ ————————————

2–3 spring onions (leaves and bulbs)
1 teaspoon bottled minced coriander
½ teaspoon bottled vinegared mint

———————————— ◆ ————————————

Finely chop the spring onions, then mix all the ingredients together. Add just enough water to make the mixture cohesive.

Orange Coconut Chutney

—— SERVES 2 ——

Coconut is soothing, but the red chilli and tomato ketchup that give this chutney its 'orange' colour also add piquancy.

———————————— ◆ ————————————

½ teaspoon black onion seeds
4 tablespoons desiccated coconut
1 tablespoon coconut milk powder

4 tablespoons milk
1 teaspoon bottled minced red chilli
1 teaspoon tomato ketchup

———————————— ◆ ————————————

Mix the onion seeds, dessicated coconut and coconut milk powder with the milk. Leave to soak for 10 minutes, then mix in the chilli and ketchup.

Onion Balti Chutney

—— SERVES 2 ——

This bright green onion chutney needs help from green food colouring as well as green ingredients.

2–3 spring onions (leaves only), very finely chopped

½ teaspoon bottled vinegared mint

1 tablespoon very finely chopped green pepper

2–3 drops green food colouring liquid

Mix all the ingredients together in a non-metallic bowl. Chill if you have time, or serve at once.

Cachumber Salad Chutney

—— SERVES 2 ——

Because this chutney consists mainly of fresh, raw onion, it is one of the best accompaniments to curry as it 'cuts' through the rich sauces.

2oz (50g) onion, thinly sliced

1 teaspoon finely chopped red pepper

½ teaspoon finely chopped fresh green chilli

½ teaspoon bottled vinegared mint

1 tablespoon fresh lemon juice

½ teaspoon paprika

Mix all the ingredients together and serve.

Balti Red Raita

—— SERVES 2 ——

Bright red yoghurt chutney has become the traditional accompaniment to Birmingham's balti dishes.

6 tablespoons Greek yoghurt
1 teaspoon tandoori curry powder (see page 8)
½ teaspoon tomato purée

1 teaspoon tomato ketchup
⅓ teaspoon dried mint
½ teaspoon bottled minced red chilli (optional)

Mix all the ingredients and chill if you have time, or serve at once.

Tandoori Green Raita

—— SERVES 2 ——

Green yoghurt chutney contrasts well with red tandooris and tikkas.

6 tablespoons Greek yoghurt
½ teaspoon bottled minced coriander
½ teaspoon bottled vinegared mint
2 teaspoons finely chopped green pepper

½ teaspoon finely chopped fresh green chilli
6–8 drops green food colouring liquid (optional)

Mix all the ingredients together in a non-metallic bowl and chill if you have time, or serve at once.

108

Curry Yellow Raita

—— SERVES 2 ——

This one needs a wee bit of work for best results – the turmeric and seeds must be fried.

---

1 tablespoon sesame oil
½ teaspoon mustard seeds
½ teaspoon turmeric
1 tablespoon finely chopped yellow
  pepper

½ teaspoon liquid yellow food
  colouring (optional)
6 tablespoons Greek yoghurt

---

1. Heat the oil in a frying pan. Fry the mustard seeds and turmeric for 10 seconds, then take off the heat and put into a bowl.

2. Add the remaining ingredients, stir well and allow to cool.

3. Chill if you have time, or serve at once.

White Coconut Raita

—— SERVES 2 ——

This mixture of yoghurt and coconut is as cool an accompaniment to curry as its white colour suggests.

---

5 tablespoons Greek yoghurt
1 tablespoon double cream
1 tablespoon desiccated coconut

2 tablespoons coconut milk powder
1 teaspoon sesame seeds

Mix all the ingredients together and chill if you have time, or serve at once.

Garam Brown Raita

—— SERVES 2 ——

The addition of garam masala to yoghurt creates a pretty beige colour and a gorgeous aromatic flavour.

———————————— ◆ ————————————

6 tablespoons Greek yoghurt
1 tablespoon garam masala (see page 6)

———————————— ◆ ————————————

Mix all the ingredients together and chill if you have time, or serve at once.

Green Chilli Chutney

—— SERVES 2 ——

I personally can't live without this. It is easy to make and keeps indefinitely. There are two points to bear in mind. One: its bright green colour 'fades' over time but the flavour remains unchanged. Two: watch where you put your hands after chopping the chillies. They can be killers if you touch your eyes after handling them. Some people prefer to wear kitchen gloves when chopping chillies, as they can make your fingertips burn too.

———————————— ◆ ————————————

4oz (110g) fresh green chillies, de-stalked and chopped
4fl oz (100ml) vinegar (any type)

———————————— ◆ ————————————

Put the chillies into an electric blender. Add the vinegar and pulse to a purée. Store in an airtight jar.

Red Chilli Chutney

—— **SERVES 2** ——

This variation of Green Chilli Chutney (opposite) uses red chillies. The same comments apply.

◆

4oz (110g) fresh red chillies, de-stalked and chopped
4fl oz (100ml) vinegar (any type)

◆

Put the chillies into an electric blender. Add the vinegar and pulse to a purée. Store in an airtight jar.

APPENDIX 1

◆

THE CURRY CLUB

Pat Chapman always had a deep-rooted interest in spicy food, curry in particular, and over the years he built up a huge pool of information which he felt could be usefully passed on to others. He conceived the idea of forming an organization for this purpose.

Since it was founded in January 1982, **The Curry Club** has built up a membership of several thousands. We have a marchioness, some lords and ladies, knights a-plenty, a captain of industry or two, generals, admirals and air marshals (not to mention a sprinkling of ex-colonels), and we have celebrity names – actresses, politicians, rock stars and sportsmen. We have an airline (Air India), a former Royal Navy warship (HMS *Hermes*) and a hotel chain (the Taj group).

We have fifteen members whose name is Curry or Currie, twenty called Rice and several with the name Spice or Spicer, Cook, Fry, Frier or Fryer and one Boiling. We have a Puri (a restaurant owner), a Paratha and a Nan and a good many Mills and Millers, one Dal and a Lentil, an Oiler, a Gee (but no Ghee), and a Butter but no Marj (several Marjories though, and a Marjoram and a Minty). We also have several Longs and Shorts, Thins and Broads, one Fatt and one Wide, and a Chilley and a Coole.

We have members on every continent including a good number of Asian members, but by and large the membership is a typical cross-section of the Great British Public, ranging in age from teenage to dotage, and in occupation from refuse collectors to receivers, high street traders to high court judges, tax inspectors to taxi drivers. There are students and pensioners, millionaires and unemployed ... thousands of people who have just one thing in common – a love of curry and spicy foods.

Members receive a bright and colourful quarterly magazine which has regular features on curry and the curry lands. It includes news items, recipes, reports on restaurants, picture features, and contributions from members and professionals alike. The information is largely concerned with curry, but by popular demand it now includes regular input on other exotic and spicy cuisines such as those of the Middle East and China. We produce a wide selection of publications, including the books listed opposite the title page.

Obtaining some of the ingredients required for curry cooking can be difficult, but The Curry Club makes it easy, with a comprehensive range of Curry Club products, including spice mixes, chutneys, pickles, popadoms, sauces and curry pastes. These are available from major food stores and specialist delicatessens up and down the country. If they are not stocked near you, there is the Club's well-established and efficient mail-order service. Hundreds of items are stocked, including spices, pickles, pastes, dry foods, tinned foods, gift items, publications and specialist kitchen and tableware.

On the social side, the Club holds residential weekend cookery courses and gourmet nights at selected restaurants. Top of the list, is our regular Curry Club gourmet trip to India and other spicy countries. We take a small group of curry enthusiasts to the chosen country and tour the incredible sights, in between sampling the delicious foods of each region.

If you would like more information about The Curry Club, write (enclosing a stamped addressed envelope please) to: **The Curry Club, PO Box 7, Haslemere, Surrey GU27 1EP.**

THE STORE CUPBOARD

The lists which follow include all the non-perishable items used in the 100 recipes in this book. Some items are used in only one recipe; others crop up again and again. The list of spices, in particular, looks formidable but it does not cost much to buy all of them and doing so can be fun. Many of the ingredients, spices included, are available from supermarkets and delicatessens. There may even be an Asian grocer near you.

Perversely, however, you are unlikely to get everything at one stop. That's where our mail-order service comes in useful (see Appendix 1 for address).

SPICES

Whole Spices

Bay leaves (*Tej patia*)
Cardamom brown/black (*Elaichi motti*)
Cardamom green (*Elaichi hari*)
Cassia bark (*Dalchini chino*)
Cinnamon stick (*Dalchini*)
Clove (*Lavang*)
Coriander seeds (*Dhania*)
Cummin seeds white (*Jeera*)
Cummin seeds black (*Kala jeera*)
Curry leaves (*Neempatta* or
   Kari phulia)

Fennel seeds (*Soonf*)
Fenugreek leaves (*Tej methi kasoori*)
Fenugreek seeds (*Methi dhana*)
Lovage seeds (*Ajowan*)
Mustard seeds brown / black (*Rai*)
Peppercorns, black (*Kala mirch*)
Poppy seeds, white (*Cuscus*)
Saffron stamens (*Zafran*)
Sesame seeds, white (*Til*)
Star anise (*Badain* or *Kakraphol*)
Wild onion seeds or nigella (*Kalonji*)

Ground spices

Asafoetida (*Hing*)
Chilli powder (*Lal mirch*)
Chilli powder, extra hot or cayenne
Cinnamon powder (*Dalchini*)
Clove, ground (*Lavang*)
Coriander, ground (*Dhania*)

Cummin, ground (*Jeera*)
Garlic powder (*Lasan*)
Mango powder (*Am chur*)
Paprika (*Paprika*)
Saffron powder (*Zafran*)
Turmeric (*Haldi*)

Fresh herbs in pots

Basil
Chives

Coriander
Mint

Oils

Butter ghee
  and/or vegetable ghee
Sesame oil
Soya oil
  and/or sunflower oil

Vegetable oil
Hazelnut oil
  and/or olive oil
  and/or pistachio nut oil

General

Almonds
  flaked
  ground
  whole
  shelled
  unsalted
Breadcrumbs
Cashew nuts
  whole
  shelled
  unsalted
Coconut
  creamed
  block
  desiccated
  unsweetened, milk powder
Lentils
  red
  split and polished

Mint dried
Mustard
  powder
  English
Onion flakes
  dried
  dried and fried
Rice
  basmati
  polished
Sugar
  dark muscovado
  white
Tomato ketchup
  purée
  soup, granulated powder
Vinegar (any type)

Bottled Items

Basil, minced
Beetroot in vinegar
Brinjal (aubergine) pickle (Indian)
Coriander, minced
Chilli, red, minced
Chilli pickle (Indian)
Food colouring liquid
  green
  red
  yellow
Garlic
  minced
  dried slices

Ginger
  minced
  dried slices
Green peppercorns in brine
Hoisin sauce
Horseradish sauce
Lemon grass stalks
Lemon or lime juice, sharp
Lime pickle (Indian)
Mango chutney
Mango pickle (Indian)

Mustard
    Dijon
    English
Peanut butter
Prawn ballichow pickle (Indian)

Soy sauce
    dark
    light
Worcestershire sauce

Canned Items

Chick peas
Humous
Lychees
Mushroom soup, cream of
Onion soup (French)
Pineapple
Potatoes
Ratatouille

Red kidney beans
Tomato
    plum
    soup, cream of
Vegetables
    mixed, diced
Vichyssoise (or cream of leek and potato soup)

INDEX

ABOUT THE AUTHOR

PAT CHAPMAN is passionate about curries and has distilled a lifetime of enthusiasm to cater for curry fanatics like himself. Pat and his wife Dominique run the Curry Club, which has several thousand members. Pat produces a glossy magazine for members, and supplies spices and unusual ingredients by mail order.

Pat regularly features in the press and on national television and radio.

Pat's previous books include *Curry Club Balti Curry Cookbook, Curry Club 250 Favourite Curries and Accompaniments, 100 Favourite Tandoori Recipes, Curry Club Indian Restaurant Cookbook, Curry Club 250 Hot and Spicy Dishes, Curry Club Favourite Restaurant Curries, Pat Chapman's Chinese Restaurant Cookbook* and *The Taj Good Curry Restaurant Guide*